A BOOK OF MAN-EATERS

A BOOK OF MAN-EATERS

By

BRIGADIER-GENERAL R.G. BURTON

GYAN

Published by

Gyan Publishing House
5, Ansari Road
Daryaganj, New Delhi-110002
Phone: 011-47034999, 9811692060
E-mail: books@gyanbooks.com

Distribution Network
gyanbooks.com
India, USA, Canada, UK, Australia, France

ISBN : 978-81-212-6711-3 (PB)
First Published, 1931

2nd Impression 2022

Printed at: Gyan Press, Delhi.

A BOOK OF MAN-EATERS
Author: BRIGADIER-GENERAL R.G. BURTON

A BOOK OF MAN-EATERS

by

Brigadier-General R. G. BURTON

Author of
"Sport and Wild Life in the Deccan," "A History of the Hyderabad Contingent," "Napoleon's Campaigns in Italy," "From Boulogne to Austerlitz," "Napoleon's Invasion of Russia," etc.

ILLUSTRATED

SECOND IMPRESSION

INTRODUCTION

THIS book is not written "to lay a literary ghost," for I have no wish to exorcise the wild beasts that haunt my waking hours and walk into the jungles of my dreams. They are pleasant companions—the tigers that prowl in the paths of sleep and are recalled daily by the travel-stained maps and by striped skins and heads, the trophies of by-gone years; the leopards that creep through the enchanted forests of my youth, and come to life again in walks abroad and in visions by the library fire; and the bears that range the pine and snow-clad mountains of memory which, as the Chinese proverb says, "are not as high as they were in the days when we were young." That they should be followed by the lions, jaguars, and pumas which, alas! I have never seen except behind the bars of a cage, is perhaps natural. For they too have been conjured up in imagination in expeditions that were never realised. But the experiences of great hunters, of Gordon Cumming, William Cotton Oswell, Samuel Baker, and Selous are recorded with those of others in the many volumes on the book-shelf, and in their fine company I have journeyed to the sources of the Nile, over the wide veldt and across the Zambesi, and wandered through the Athi plains into the wilds of Central Africa.

Scattered in those volumes, as well as in the pages of memory from an old hunter's experience, many man-eaters are to be met with. But it is not possible for one man to come into contact with more than a few man-killing carnivorous monsters, for such are rare and abnormal. In this volume, therefore, I not only sink the string of thought into the well of memory, but lay under contribution the tales and records of sportsmen and others for stories that are here related. Many of these episodes are instinct with human tragedy, and possess a remarkable and often dramatic fascination. Moreover, there are many popular misconceptions regarding the nature of wild beasts, every great cat, wolf, hyena, crocodile, and shark, and sometimes even the harmless bear, being regarded as an actual or potential man-eater. For this some early hunters and writers of fiction are largely to blame, and it is well that such erroneous ideas should be dispelled, and that the history of man-eating wild beasts should be placed in its true perspective.

Although this book is designed to deal mainly with carnivorous animals in their capacity of man-eaters, it has been thought advisable, and indeed essential, to give some account of the distribution, habits, and character of these wild beasts, as well as of the methods of hunting them. While these matters are of interest in themselves, there may be something new to say on the subject and some light may be thrown on various questions connected with it, such as the senses of scent and sight, the causes of wild beasts taking to man-eating, the degree of protection afforded by camp-fires, and the man-eater's habits in relation to the seizure of its victim. With some knowledge of these things the reader will be able to appreciate the nature of particular animals which have taken to preying on human beings.

Recently an enterprising lady was about to accompany her husband on an expedition into the heart of Africa, an adventure already accomplished by other ladies. It was implied that she was engaging in a very dangerous undertaking, and would be in grave and contínous peril from wild men and wild beasts. She will probably be safer in Africa than in England, where some 7000 people were killed and 170,000 injured in road accidents in 1930; such traffic dangers will be avoided in the heart of Africa, where the rhinoceros has something of the impetus of a motor-car but is much less dangerous. Then there is less prospect of being murdered in Africa than in England, and certainly much less than in the United States of America, where the annual murder bill amounts to some 12,000 human beings. Murders of white people in Africa are exceedingly rare. And in Africa the traveller will find a happier people, leading a freer life than, and in their own way enjoying as high a standard of living as, the inhabitants of civilized countries; for they have fewer and simpler wants and less to make them envious of others.

With regard to India we cannot be so certain. Fifty, forty, and even twenty years ago white people, especially ladies, might travel alone from one end of India to the other without fear of hurt or molestation; they would have met with nothing but courtesy and consideration from a gentle people whose minds had not been poisoned by Western politics, whose pathetic contentment had not yet been disturbed, and whose Arcadian simplicity of life might well be the envy of the less fortunate peoples of Europe.

But in all countries dangers from wild beasts are so

slight that they may be ignored unless the traveller looks for trouble by attacking the more pugnacious animals. Most animals, even lions, tigers, leopards, bears, and wolves, avoid the presence of man and retreat before his approach. Many wild beasts have in the past been greatly maligned, and represented as monsters which regard man as a deadly enemy to be attacked at sight, as in truth they might not without reason regard him. We read much of man's inhumanity to man, his cruelty to animals has if possible attained wider dimensions.

Wild beasts do not generally go about seeking whom they might devour. The carnivora have no special taste for human flesh, which is perhaps as unpleasant and repulsive to most of them as the flesh of the carnivora is to us. Dog does not eat dog! though it must be acknowledged that dog is the favourite food of the leopard, the hyena, and the wolf. But when a carnivorous animal takes to man-eating it is terrible and relentless; its contact with human beings appears to sharpen its wits and augment its natural stealth and cunning; it is swift and ferocious in attack; in its search for human prey it travels far throughout the area it infests and becomes a terror to the countryside. It has cultivated an insatiable desire for human flesh, which may be imparted to its descendants. It is with the character of those species, of which individuals are addicted to preying on human beings, that this volume is mainly concerned.

I had occasion recently to mention in another place that I had picketed out live buffalo calves as bait for tigers, this being the only method by which the tiger could be marked down and shot. This brought me an anonymous post-card from an indignant lady, who wrote: "How horrible and disgusting of you to picket out a live animal to be devoured by a ferocious beast, and this done for what you call sport. You ought to be picketed out yourself!" I commend this volume to her notice. If she had seen husband or child seized, dragged off into the jungle, and devoured by a wild beast, and possibly heard the crunching of the victim's bones, she would not have been so indignant at the sacrifice of a calf, whose death, moreover, saved the lives of some hundreds of its own kind. The annual mortality due to wild beasts in India amounts to some 3000 human beings.

My acknowledgments are due to big-game hunters, many of whom have gone to the Happy Hunting Grounds, for their contributions to the subject of this book; and to the Bombay Natural History Society, whose Journal is a mine of valuable information.

R. G. BURTON.

CONTENTS

CHAPTER III

CHAPTER IV

CHAPTER V

A BOOK OF MAN-EATERS

A BOOK OF MAN-EATERS

CHAPTER I

MAN-EATERS

THERE is not only a very human interest but a strange and awful fascination in the history of man-eaters, of which there are many species, including man himself, who, however, generally eats only his enemies, and often has behind the eating a spiritual or religious motive. But it is not proposed here to deal at length with cannibals, although they must find place in a comprehensive view of the subject. Nor will those numerous creatures which feed upon the dead be dealt with in detail. Dead human flesh is regarded by carrion feeders and scavengers like any other flesh; they do not discriminate. The vultures that appear like specks in the sky and soon gather over and descend upon the dead on the field of battle, or on the wayfarer who, from the exhaustion of famine or disease, sinks in death upon his journey; the jackals, hyenas, sharks and other fish, lobsters, crabs, and various crustaceans devour the corpses of man and of all other animals that come in their way. In the West Indies, where we used to hunt land-crabs by night with nooses on sticks, these creatures, esteemed a delicacy, are said to have a special predilection for residence in graveyards. We did not seek them there! During the Peninsular War an officer recorded that he saw the corpses of French soldiers after one of the battles of the Pyrenees being eaten by great trout in the river into which they had fallen. Those who have seen the drowned washed up on the shore know how these are dealt with by the scavengers of the sea.

In days gone by, in time of famine and cholera epidemics from which India has been largely relieved by a beneficent English government, the victims of disease and starvation used to die in thousands by the wayside and in the jungles. They were devoured by hyenas, jackals, dogs, vultures, crows, and sometimes by the great marabout storks, known as adjutant-birds, which are useful scavengers in Calcutta and other cities, where in former times they contended with pariah dogs and kites for scraps of offal. But these storks occasionally reach Southern India, where I have seen them feeding on the bodies of bison killed the day before. Troops on the march, both English and Indian, used to suffer terribly from cholera, owing to the pollution of the water supply, when the cause of the disease was unknown. Numerous graves by the wayside mark the last resting-place of the forgotten dead on roads where now for many years the echoes that were once awakened by the tramp of marching troops, the beat of drums, and the sound of bugles, are for ever silent. These victims of cholera found at least a decent burial.

Far otherwise with the miserable wayfarers during the epidemics which spread over and devastated the towns and villages. An officer who marched from Nagpur to Bhusawal before the construction of the railway during a terrible epidemic observed signs of the presence of death along the road. In the vicinity of the small hamlets were newly covered graves with the foul clothes of the dead lying beside them, evidence of pestilence in its most hideous form. From these shallow graves corpses might be seen lying about, dragged out by jackals and village dogs, the skulls yet covered with long matted hair.

In times of famine the countryside used to be littered with skulls and other human remains. People wandered from their homes in the vain hope of finding food elsewhere, or of reaching relief works, or even to seek for a miserable sustenance in jungle tracts. In 1900 we observed many human remains in the waste grounds of the Deccan. I recollect one morning when out for a ride putting up a jackal from the skeleton of a human being lying a few yards from a pool of muddy water. It was a famine year of drought which had not only destroyed the growing crops but had dried up almost the whole of the water supply in that part of the country. Even in the deep wells of the cantonment there was scarcely enough to provide for the wants of the troops, and the river was no more than a dry bed. The skeleton, incarnadined with blood in the light of the rising sun, had been stripped of flesh by foul beasts during the night that was just over, and now lay with bony arms extended towards the water which he had never reached. The wayfarer's staff and miserable scrap of clothing lay where they had fallen. Water might have enabled him to totter to the place, a mile or so farther on, where he would have found relief, but he had not strength to reach it. It was a tragedy typical of many of which there was evidence in the skulls scattered over the jungle and the waste.

In view of these occurrences, and of the habit of burying bodies in shallow graves instead of burning them in times of pestilence, it is not surprising that in some districts in India the prevalence of man-eating tigers and leopards has been ascribed to their having acquired a taste for human flesh through feeding on the dead, who have thus strewn the country in seasons of drought and famine, where they have died, unknelled, uncoffined, and unknown. In such times of calamity there is often a dearth of water in whole districts; cattle and deer die in thousands; the usual prey of carnivorous animals becomes scarce, and it is possible that tigers and leopards may have seized dying, enfeebled, or sleeping sufferers who often wander into the jungles in search of berries and roots, or of the shoots and seeds of the bamboo, the blossoms of the mohwa, and other wild products which may be observed to be scattered with a more lavish hand than usual by beneficent Nature in times of drought and scarcity. But tigers and leopards are not fond of carrion, although they will feed on a very high carcass of their own killing. They will eat animals found dead, but it is improbable that they have begun a career of man-eating by feasting on quickly decaying human corpses. Statistics might reveal whether there has been an increase in the mortality from wild beasts during or after a famine year.

Crocodiles and turtles feed on the corpses which are thrown in thousands into the sacred waters of the Ganges and other rivers; these reptiles like their food in a high condition, although the fresh bodies of cats and ducks may be found in the stomachs of crocodiles. At the burning ghats where the dead are cremated on funeral pyres on the banks of the Mahi river in Western India, the relatives of the deceased attending the funeral leave the scene when the wood is well alight. But before it has burnt out and while the embers are still glowing, great turtles and crocodiles rush from the water as soon as the people have departed. In their eagerness they plunge into the embers to seize portions of the corpse, so indifferent to the heat that the skin can be seen curling up on their backs as they hurry off to the cooling waters, bearing an arm, a leg, or a chunk of flesh in their ravening maws.

But the principal man-eaters are those dread carnivorous beasts which attack living man in preference or in addition to what is generally regarded as their natural prey. These are, in Europe, the wolf; in Africa, the lion, leopard, crocodile, and hyena; in Asia, the lion, tiger, leopard, wolf, hyena, and crocodile, and occasionally the python; in America, the jaguar, puma, and alligator, and rarely the anaconda and boa-constrictor The reasons for including bears, which are not really man-eaters, are given in the chapter relating to those animals. Of Indian provinces, Bengal, although it has been called "the paradise of nations," is the greatest sufferer from the depredations of savage beasts. In one year it had a mortality of nearly 12,000 human beings and the same number of cattle, due to wild animals and snakes.

There is a widespread popular notion that man-eating lions and tigers are always animals disabled by age or other causes, and it used to be thought that their feeding on human flesh induced a mangy condition. It will be seen from examples given in this volume that many man-eaters are old animals, often with defective teeth, or sometimes suffering from wounds or other injuries. Indeed, the few cases of recovery of those attacked have usually been due to absent or worn-down teeth of the animal. Such disabilities have made it difficult for them to kill their ordinary prey, or to break up and eat a thick-skinned carcass ; they find man, seized unawares, an easy prey, devoured without difficulty, and they thus acquire a craving for human flesh which is as nourishing as that of any other animal. At the same time pain may render animals savage, aggressive, and ready to attack when disturbed by man ; pain is a source of ill-temper in many human beings. But in numerous instances man-eaters have been strong and vigorous beasts in the prime of life.

Man-eating lions and tigers tend to frequent particular districts, and this has been in some quarters ascribed to a hereditary taint. That it may be hereditary in the sense of being passed on in a family is probable, not as a taint in the blood, but by practice and example, for acquired characteristics are not inherited. There is a general preponderance of females among man-eaters. They are probably in the first instance driven to this practice by the difficulty of finding sufficient food for themselves and their young. Once adopted, they find man-killing comparatively easy, whether the difficulty has been due to a scarcity of game or cattle, or to disablement from wounds or infirmity. Gautama Buddha, moved by pity for all living things, and following his own noble doctrine :

> Kill not, for pity's sake, and lest ye slay
> The meanest thing upon its upward way,

surrendered himself a willing victim to the starving

tigress "at whose poor lean dugs two cubs, whining with famine, tugged and sucked, mumbling those milk-less teats which rendered nought." And so he stepped forth, and the perishing beast hurled him to the earth and had her feast of him :

> With all the crooked daggers of her claws
> Rending his flesh, and all her yellow fangs
> Bathed in his blood : the great cat's burning breath
> Mixed with the last sigh of such fearless love.

But had the Buddha been aware of it, or considered human life of more value than that of tigers, he might have appreciated the danger to generations of human beings in thus affording these beasts a taste for the flesh of man, which they might pass on to their descendants by education and example.

It is probably due to this method of transmission that the prevalence of man-eating lions and tigers in particular areas and persisting over prolonged periods has been observed, as in the case of the lions of Sanga, where a reign of terror existed for some years, with an appalling death roll, and of tigers in the neighbourhood of Bombay some fifty to sixty years ago. The same thing has occurred in the district of Sironcha in the Central Provinces, where Lieutenant R. S. Burton destroyed two infamous man-eating tigers in 1930, and where he says man-eaters appear to be "hereditary," infesting the country for a considerable period. Animals with this propensity prefer human flesh to other food.

Among the causes of the carnivora taking to man-killing is the depletion of game which furnishes their natural prey. This in the first place induces a resort to domesticated animals for food, and leads to closer familiarity with and discovery of the helplessness of man, who in course of time is likely to fall a victim himself, sometimes in the first instance owing to the accidental killing of a herdsman protecting his flocks from attack. But such an accident need not necessarily awaken a desire for human victims. A tiger shot at Patoda in the Deccan had killed a herdsman who tried to drive it from his cattle; but the tiger did not eat him nor did it kill anyone else. A leopard shot in the same part of the country killed a woman who, when collecting wood, came upon it suddenly but it left the body untouched.

I have known more than one instance of a tiger or leopard tasting the blood of man without acquiring any appetite for human prey. In 1898 a tiger lay up in a garden in the cantonment of Jalna in the Deccan, out of which it was driven and wounded by a shot in the hind-leg. It escaped in the darkness and made its way some miles out into a cultivated district. Here some days later I came upon the spot where it had a few hours before seized and mortally wounded a villager employed in scaring birds in a field of millet, the stalks of which, some six feet high, afforded the tiger complete concealment. The tiger had at once left the man without any attempt to eat him, although the victim, bitten through the body and almost disembowelled, was unable to move and died a few hours after he was found. He told me that he heard a peculiar noise, and on going to the place was attacked by the wild beast. In this instance the tiger might well have devoured the victim, for when we tracked him down and shot him next day, he was in a starved and emaciated condition, having had no food for at least a week, while he was also suffering from a painful wound.

Perhaps there is a natural repugnance to human flesh as food, due to the fact that man as well as the tiger is a carnivorous animal. This cannot, however, be the whole reason for the general immunity of man, or man-eaters would be such only when driven by extremity of hunger; but it may be an acquired taste. Moreover, although the carnivora prey mainly on graminivorous animals, they eat other flesh-eaters on occasion. Both tigers and lions have been known to devour their own species; tigers will eat bears and leopards; leopard will eat leopard, and hyenas, leopards, and wolves have a special predilection for dog.

Beasts of prey may seize human beings by accident or mistake. I recollect a goatherd, lying asleep wrapped in a black blanket in the shadow of a bush, being seized by a leopard in broad daylight. The animal at once relinquished its capture without having done much harm; it is probable that the man in a blanket both smelt and looked like one of his own goats. An accident of a different kind, but due to a similar cause, led to a more tragic result in Kashmir, where a sportsman, seeing what he took to be a bear lying among bushes on the hillside, fired at and killed it. The corpse was that of an old woman wrapped in a blanket. A village jury assessed the amount of compensation for the relatives at fourpence!

The question of a natural fear of man in wild animals is discussed in the next chapter. The great carnivora approach their human and other prey by stealth. If boldly faced, the man-eater will often retreat. But the human being seldom faces his destroyer; he is seized unawares either by the throat when lying asleep or from behind by the back of the neck in the daytime. The legend of the supposed power of the human eye may have arisen from this circumstance, or it may be due to the prevalent idea that wild beasts are always ready to attack man and to ignorance of the fact that an animal which is not a man-eater seldom molests a human being.

Reluctance to face man is a remarkable feature in attacks by man-eaters. That man seldom sees his assailant is illustrated by many instances, such as men who have recovered after being seized and those who have seen the beast when it was about to attack and so have escaped seizure; especially significant is the case where the tigress, having dropped a corpse in a sitting position against a bank, unable to get at her prey from behind, would not approach and face the staring eyes. Another interesting point in the habits of man-eating lions and tigers is their reluctance to leave their human prey when once seized, as in the case of the tiger that carried off Munro on Sagar Island, the tigress that attacked Mr. George, and the lion that killed O'Hara and afterwards prowled all night round the tent where the corpse lay.

Another subject of interest and importance to travellers and sportsmen is that of the protection afforded by camp-fires, the general impression being that fire in itself will keep wild beasts at a distance. This is dealt with in subsequent chapters, and the reader can draw his conclusions from facts which should dissipate prevalent misconceptions. As for the methods of hunting by the great carnivora, whether by scent, hearing or sight, or the use of all three senses, it makes little difference to the victim of the man-eater how he is hunted, but it is important as it may influence his actions. The Tsavo lions on one occasion took a bag of rice instead of one of fourteen coolies in the same tent, and another night preferred a mattress to the man who was lying on it. But it would be unwise to infer that the lion has deficient powers of sight or scent. The lion and tiger are quick to see a moving object, but slow in making out a stationary object. Whether the lion's mistake in seizing these objects instead of the prey was due to an error of sight or scent cannot be known; but Professor G. M. Robertson throws much light on the subject of the senses of the carnivora when he tells us that "the intelligent interpretation of what is seen is very poor in animals."

CHAPTER II

THE FEAR OF MAN IN WILD ANIMALS

IT is generally accepted that wild animals have a natural fear of man, and it is often supposed that this fear is the chief reason why all the great carnivora are not man-eaters, and why the propensity for preying on human beings is confined to comparatively few individuals of certain species. The fact that most wild beasts refrain from attacking man on all occasions, whether for the purpose of eating him or otherwise, is too frequently ascribed to the same reason; while a still wider public holds the popular notion that lions, tigers, leopards, wolves, and even bears behave as if they were the enemies of mankind, and attack whenever opportunity offers.

The truth is that wild beasts, even of the most bloodthirsty kind, rarely molest man, whether this be due to inborn fear or to other causes. It is therefore interesting to enquire into the subject of this chapter, and attempt to discover whether there are grounds for supposing that wild animals generally are born with a natural fear of human beings, or whether such fear is due to experience and possibly to heredity. Men also are afraid without reason, for the lion, tiger, or leopard will usually get out of the way as soon as possible in ninety-nine cases out of a hundred. Even when a man-eater is in the way, it will take care not to show itself; it will not face man openly, but approach and seize its prey unawares, so stealthily that the victim is not likely to look upon the face of death. The beast will not generally take its victim, human or otherwise, if aware that it is observed. The man-eater seen by its prospective prey retreats. The herdsman seldom sees the tiger or leopard that destroys his cattle, even when they are taken in daylight; it is the straggler that falls a prey. The history of man-eaters, into which so much human tragedy enters, as it does in the cases of violence and murder which furnish so curious an attraction to many people, would probably be still more fascinating if it were generally understood that man-eaters among carnivorous animals are as rare as murderers among human beings.

It is a libel on the tiger to speak of it as the embodiment of cruelty. The lion or tiger is less cruel than man himself. These animals do not assemble in armies to attack their own kind. They kill only for food or in defence of themselves or their young, and generally kill cleanly and without the infliction of much suffering. Man indeed, in view of his history, has little cause to stigmatise the tiger as cruel. In killing his fellow-creatures he has not even the excuse that he kills for food. When he does so, as has occasionally happened in the case of shipwrecked sailors who have devoured their own kind in order to sustain life, he has generally been excused. But even in the destruction of human beings, leaving war out of the question, man has nothing to boast of in comparison with wild animals.

In India over a series of years the victims of wild beasts numbered as many as 3000 each year, in addition to some 20,000 killed by poisonous snakes. The victims of wild beasts were with few exceptions killed for food or by animals acting in self-defence. Even the serpent bites not from malice but for self-protection. For purposes of comparison the victims of murder in a highly civilized country may be considered. In the United States of America these amount to about 12,000 a year, or roughly one to every 9000 of the population; that is, four times the number of human beings killed by wild beasts in India, which has a population more than three times as great, are murdered every year in the United States. If we add the victims of snakes in India, it is found that, in proportion to the population, human beings are far more destructive of human life in the States than are all the Indian wild beasts and snakes together.

Wild beasts in general seek their prey among wild animals, although large numbers of domesticated animals are killed by lions, tigers, leopards, and wolves. In one year 50,000 cattle were reported killed by wild beasts in India, but the number must have greatly exceeded this. Even in this respect there is more destruction by man, and with less excuse; vegetarian races, to say nothing of anthropoid apes, stand as evidence that man can thrive without a carnivorous diet; the great cats and the wolves cannot; yet in the United Kingdom 40,000 animals are slaughtered daily for food, many thousands in the most horrible manner. In hunting wild beasts, man pursues his game more for pleasure than for food. No doubt the carnivora are terrible in attack and, like normal man, find a pleasure in the hunt, but with them the motive of self-preservation in the struggle for existence is always present; they can sustain life only on flesh and blood. The carnassial teeth of man are as undeveloped as those of the ape, which points to his having been originally a frugivorous animal. His carnivorous propensities are acquired rather than inborn, and some of the finest races of India, such as the Rajputs and Jats, are mainly vegetarian. If wild animals have a fear of man, acquired by inherited experience, there is ample reason for it.

It is remarkable that carnivorous animals do not in general prey on man, for under natural conditions most wild animals have appeared to have no fear of the human race, and unarmed man is an easy prey. Fear seems to be an acquired rather than an inherited characteristic. Very young wild animals exhibit no special fear of man, whether they be lions, tigers, leopards, bears, or fledgling birds, which will take food from the hand but show alarm when they are nearly ready to leave the nest. Darwin says that in England "even nestling birds fear man," although elsewhere in the same book (*The Voyage of the Beagle*) he tells us that fear is not a natural instinct but an inherited habit, and illustrates this with examples from his own experience during his travels. In places where man has been hitherto unknown, his presence is no more productive of fear or apprehension than is that of other living things.

Darwin observed that the capybaras which frequented the islands at the mouth of the river Plata and in other localities were very tame, especially at Maldonada where, by cautious stalking, he approached within three yards of four old ones. He accounted for this tameness by the jaguar having been banished for some years, and by the Gaucho not thinking it worth while to hunt them. Whether the presence of jaguars would make capybaras more timid in the presence of man is open to question; it might make them generally suspicious; capybaras are abundant in the islands of the Rio Parana, where they form the usual prey of the jaguar. Darwin also found the deer in Patagonia not merely tame but inquisitive, although exceedingly wary when approached on horseback. In that country no one goes on foot, and the deer knows man as its enemy only when mounted and armed with the bolas. He also found that the animals did not fear the report of a gun. In India spotted deer are inquisitive; I recollect coming upon a herd of hinds which, when I stood still, came walking towards me a few paces at a time, giving utterance to short, sharp barks; they will approach a beast of prey in the same manner. There seems to be no particular reason why animals should be alarmed by the report of a gun any more than by any other sudden noise. In forests the sound of the axe is not uncommonly heard; often one reads of the "boldness" of leopards returning to a kill shortly after being fired at and missed once or twice, but the animal cannot be aware that a projectile has been fired at it, or that an attempt has been made on its life, although it is naturally startled by an unwonted noise. There is a tendency to ascribe to animals human modes of thought and apprehension.

Birds are easily tamed. Those species that prey on insect parasites in the jaws of crocodiles, on ticks on the backs of bison where they may be seen riding on a herd moving through the forest, and the egrets sitting on the backs of cattle in India, do not fear to seek food on the bodies of their hosts. In the same way wild birds may be tamed to take food from the hand of man, of whom they have no fear where they have not been disturbed. In the Galapagos Islands, Darwin found a gun almost superfluous, and with the muzzle he pushed a hawk off the branch of a tree. One day a mocking-thrush alighted on the edge of a pitcher which he held in his hand, and began very quietly to sip the water; it allowed him to lift it from the ground when seated on the vessel. In Charles Island he saw a boy sitting by a well with a switch in his hand with which he killed the doves and finches as they came to drink.

Three hundred and fifty years ago, Du Bois found all the birds on the Island of Bourbon, with the exception of geese and flamingoes, so tame that they could be caught by the hand or killed in any number with a stick. The geese and flamingoes, being migratory, had probably been hunted elsewhere, and so had acquired a dread of man. Geese, so wild and difficult to approach, are comparatively tame when they first arrive in Northern India from their summer haunts in Central Asia. In a boat on the Sutlej one may float down with the current to within easy range of a flock that has just alighted. Carmichael found that the only two land birds in Tristan d'Acunha, a thrush and a bunting, were so tame as to suffer themselves to be caught with a hand-net. Both Pernety and Darwin found the birds in the Falkland Islands exceedingly tame, including snipe, upland and lowland geese, and hawks; the latter contrasts them with the birds of Tierra del Fuego where they have been persecuted for ages past by the wild inhabitants. Cowley in 1684 noted that the turtle-doves on the Galapagos Islands were so tame that they would alight on the men's hats and arms, so that they were able to take them alive, "they not fearing man until such time as our company did fire at them, whereby they were rendered more shy"; and Dampier observed that a man might in a morning's walk kill six or seven of these doves. The familiarity with which Cherry Kearton was met by the penguins of his island was of the same quality as that which led to the extinction of the great auk.

My own experience in India indicates that wild animals are easy to approach where they have not been much hunted. Darwin held that in the course of generations acquired fear becomes an inherited characteristic. Perhaps the generally held principle that acquired characters are not transmitted by heredity applies only to physical and not to mental attributes. But the theory that fear is inherited is not borne out by the behaviour of animals in captivity or under protection, unless it remains latent or is obliterated by the conditions. In sanctuaries such as deer-parks and antelope preserves, where they are not molested, animals exhibit little more fear of man than they do in the Zoological Gardens. In the game preserves of the Nizam of Hyderabad and the Gaikwar of Baroda, the antelope are practically fearless; when hunting with the cheetah, the bullock-cart on which the animal was carried was driven close up to the herd before the cheetah was unhooded and loosed at the game. In many parts of India the nilgai and the peafowl are held sacred by the Hindus and are protected accordingly; they are almost as tame as domesticated animals, but elsewhere they are among the wariest of creatures. In the Yellowstone National Park, bears and other animals neither fear nor are feared by man.

The absence of timidity on the part of the American bison led to its almost complete destruction. Whales and sea-lions are fearless in fresh localities, and the early mariners in the uncharted Arctic found a profusion of animal life which regarded man with indifference. Explorers in Africa told the same tale. They passed through countless herds of wild animals which generally exhibited no more fear than do the domesticated flocks in our fields. No human eye will again behold what Roualeyn Gordon Cumming saw eighty years ago, when he wrote: "I beheld the plains and even the hill-sides which stretched away on every side of me thickly covered not with herds, but with vast masses of springboks; as far as the eye could strain the landscape was alive with them, until they softened down into a red mass of living creatures." They were unafraid in those great solitudes, and Sir Harry Johnston forty years later observed a similar tameness in the fauna of the dense forests of Central Africa.

It is noteworthy that animals that are much hunted soon become wild and difficult to approach, while those not sought after learn that they have nothing to fear from the aggressive character of man. Selous said of the African elephant, which has always been hunted, that "it will do everything in its power to avoid meeting a human being." The bonte-quagga are not naturally very wary, and where they had not been much disturbed he found them inquisitive. In country where the Burchell's zebras had never seen a man with clothes on, Selous says these animals often came within a hundred yards to have a good look at him; on one occasion a large herd came within fifty yards of where he sat on an ant-heap, and stood staring at him for half an hour, only making off when he walked towards them; they fraternised with his horses. Buffaloes were equally unsuspicious of danger where they had not been hunted, and gazed unconcernedly at the sight of a human being, or trotted a few paces towards him to get a better sight of him. The hippopotamuses protected by Lobengula on the Umzingwani river were tame and confiding, and in many places these animals were inquisitive.

If birds and harmless ruminants do not naturally fear man, there is surely less reason for dread in the great carnivora, which are so well able to defend themselves. It would be surprising if a predaceous beast possessing the armature, cunning, and agility of the lion and tiger were cowed in the presence of a human being. When they have tried their strength against defenceless man, these creatures soon come to know that they have nothing to fear provided they take him unawares; and although a herd-boy of ten years will drive the tiger from his flocks, the man-eater soon becomes the terror of the country-side, while in the wounded beast fear is often overcome by ferocity, or dread of further injury leads to retaliation. But it seems certain that these animals in general do not attack man only because they have no taste for human flesh until they happen to become man-eaters. Fear does not enter into the question. I have come upon a leopard sitting unconcernedly by the roadside while my baggage-carts were rumbling by, and a large number of men were passing; and have nearly trodden on one lying under a bush before it made off, its presence being revealed by the smell of wild beast.

A remarkable instance of the indifference of a tiger

in such circumstances was related to me by Captain F. J. Winter, Royal Artillery, who was shooting in the Melghat Forest, in the Satpura Hills, with Mr. J. Ballantine, the Conservator of the district. They were taking an evening stroll to see if any deer were moving about in the large valley below the mountain. Going down a nullah which ended in a sheer drop of over a thousand feet directly down to this valley, they were approaching their vantage-point when they were astonished to see a fine tiger occupying their look-out or observation post. He was evidently looking for the movement of deer. They were unarmed, and the tiger did not scent their approach, or if he did, it did not disturb him. Ballantine whispered: " Look, a tiger ! " The tiger at once turned and came straight towards them; they had no means of avoiding him in the narrow nullah. Ballantine said: " Lie flat, he may pass by ! " However, when the tiger reached them, he simply leapt over their legs without uttering a sound, and disappeared slowly and leisurely. They never saw him again.

The man-eater does not attack its human prey openly, as will appear in the subsequent pages, probably not from fear, but from the natural instinct of the wild beast to approach its quarry by stealth so as not to alarm it into flight, a habit essential to success in the chase. The attack on man in this respect therefore differs in no way from that on other animals. It will approach grazing or tethered cattle in the same way, though neither man nor domesticated animals can escape by swift movement like deer and antelope.

CHAPTER III

CANNIBALS

TRACES of cannibalism are found in the early history of many races, and in Europe particularly in that of the Celts. Perhaps the legends and nursery tales of man-eating giants and ogres have their origin in such derivations, or they may be derived from the Agors, reputed to feed on the dead, whose bodies are plentiful on the banks of the sacred Ganges. Arrian tells us that the Scythians, whose drinking-bowls were the skulls of slain enemies, devoured the flesh of the dead and buried the bones in ossuaries. The early Christians were falsely accused of cannibalism, possibly owing to the primitive language of religious dogma, which persists to-day.

Cannibalism probably originated in early times in the practice of eating enemies killed in battle. Herodotus describes anthropophagy in the funeral feasts of the Medines of Central Asia, where there are no cannibals in our time ; and Othello told Desdemona of " anthropophagi and men whose heads do grow beneath their shoulders," which Shakespeare may have got from the tales of African travellers. It is said that American Indians drank the blood and ate the hearts of brave enemies in order to assimilate the virtues of the dead, as in India the liver of the tiger may be eaten to acquire the courage of the animal. The Mexicans, who attained a high standard of civilization, were addicted to cannibalism, probably from similar motives; but it fell to a modern American to partake of human flesh to satisfy, not an insatiable appetite, but a boundless curiosity. The aboriginal Australians ate their relations, especially the aged and some of the new-born, for the purpose of retaining the life of the dead in the family or tribe.

On the Amazons cannibalism was and probably still is very prevalent. Bates relates how two young half-castes of San Paulo went to trade with an Indian tribe, and had not been long gone when their canoe returned with the news that they had been shot with arrows, roasted, and eaten by savages. A party sent to make enquiries, and retaliate if necessary, found the Indian village evacuated with the exception of a girl who had been in the wood when the savages fled. She was brought back, baptized, and taught Portuguese, and she entered Bates' domestic service. He heard her relate in the coolest manner possible how she ate a portion of the bodies of the young men, while the widow of one of the victims, who happened to be present during the narrative, showed her interest by laughing at the broken Portuguese in which the girl related the horrible story.

Darwin learnt that in Tierra del Fuego the various tribes were cannibals when at war. Certainly when pressed by hunger they killed and ate their old women in preference to their dogs. Why? "Doggies catch otters, old women, no!" A boy described how they were killed by being held over smoke and choked; he imitated their screams as a joke, and described the parts of their bodies which were considered best to eat. The old women often ran away into the mountains, but were pursued and brought back to the slaughter-house at their own firesides.

The magical idea of assimilating the spirits of the dead prevailed in the human sacrifices of ancient Greece, and was no doubt of similar origin to that of the massacres carried out on the death of a king in Asia, as revealed by recent excavations, and in Africa in our time, so that the spirits of the slain might accompany their departed monarch and serve him in the next world; but cannibalism was apparently not a feature of this slaughter. But although savage tribes generally eschewed their friends and relatives as ceremonial food, they devoured their enemies. In South America they even bred a supply of human food in the offspring of captive women, expeditions being undertaken to capture them; children were thus bred as we breed animals for food. In Australia, however, they ate their new-born children, as rabbits are addicted to eating their young. All the world is kin!

In Africa cannibal tribes are now chiefly found in the forests of the Congo. These probably began in their early wars to eat enemies killed in battle, and this developed into the general practice of man-eating. Medicine-men and witch doctors kept alive the habit of cannibalism. There were Human Leopard Societies by whom victims were seized and murdered, dragged into the forest, and there eaten, the tracks of leopards being printed around where the struggle had taken place in order to deceive investigators. These pug-marks of leopards are easily made with the hand; in India a shikari had a tiger's paw cut out of wood, deceiving his employer with the imprints made by this instrument in suitable localities. Elsewhere in Africa, medicine-men claimed to be able to pick out the leopard-men, and by this means numbers of innocent unfortunates were selected and put to death. These things perhaps gave rise to the African superstition of were-leopards, people who could change themselves from human beings into man-eating leopards, which is also prevalent in some parts of India.

Captain Hayward relates[1] that a Gosha woman at Kismayu complained to him that a Nubian woman turned herself into a leopard with flaming eyes, and prowled round her hut at night. The reason given was jealousy of a man who had rejected the Nubian in favour of the Gosha. On enquiry, witnesses confirmed the complainant's statement. The Nubian had staring glassy eyes and wore a cotton cloth with curious reddish smears, which she kept hitching round her with claw-like, long-nailed hands. She walked with a feline movement. Later the Gosha was reported to have been carried off by a wild beast; Captain Hayward saw the hut where she was seized, and took the tracks to be those of a leopard. Blood in front of the door led to a gap in the thorn fence, and where the animal had broken through was a piece of cloth recognized from the red smears as that of the Nubian woman. The natives averred that she had turned herself into a leopard and carried off her rival. Neither woman was seen again.

In New Zealand the Maoris were cannibals until comparatively recent times. A typical instance of man-eating took place in the North Island in 1774, when ten men belonging to the *Adventure* were surprised on

[1] *The Mysterious Lorian Swamp*. By Captain Hayward. Seeley & Service.

shore, put to death, cooked, and eaten. A search party found first a human left hand, recognized from the initials tattooed on it as that of Thomas Hill, a seaman. Further search revealed a great assemblage of Maoris, with their canoes off-shore. They fled on the approach of the ship, which ran in close, opened fire with guns, and dispersed the natives with many killed and wounded. The landing party pursued them and came upon a fire on which were broiling the heads and portions of the bodies of four of their people; other remains with hands and limbs were lying near in a mangled condition. The canoes were destroyed and the remains buried at sea.

In the Solomon Islands cannibalism is not now practised, but was prevalent fifty years ago, when the cannibals might be seen carrying a body with the arms and legs lashed together for convenience of transport by two men, and then slung on a pole like the carcass of a pig, or of an antelope when one has been out shooting. War canoes were launched with libations of human blood collected in bowls when the victim, tied to a stake, was slashed to pieces, each cannibal selecting his cut and carving it off the living "joint." The chops and steaks were cooked in sections of bamboo on heated ironstones. A Solomon Island cannibal told Mr. Dickinson[1] that white man's flesh "did not eat much better than soap"; a black man's was like paw-paw, a delicate fruit.

I recollect observing fires burning in the wildest forest-covered mountains in 1885 when coasting round Haiti and San Domingo in the Royal Mail steamer

[1] *A Trader in the Savage Solomons*. By J. H. Dickinson. Witherby, 1927.

Moselle. The commander, Captain Jellicoe, father of the Admiral of the Great War, told me that the negroes had in some parts reverted to cannibalistic rites, so they may have been cooking their own kind over the bale-fires in the forest.

To-day, perhaps, cannibalism persists only in the Congo region of Africa and in New Guinea, and possibly in the interior of Australia. A good story is related in his book, *Kachalola*, by Dr. Broomfield, an adventurous traveller in New Guinea, four of whose carriers were carried off and devoured by cannibals. The white man was determined to avenge the murder. He with his armed men attacked the cannibal village, killed many savages, and captured others, the culprits being proved guilty by the discovery of the heads and other remains. Among the prisoners was the cannibal medicine-man. The captives were ordered to hang this villain, the chief assassin. The first man refused, and was himself hanged; another cannibal, refusing, was being pulled up on the rope when he consented, and did the job. The prisoners were made to cut down the body and hand it over to the women to cook. This was done. At first they refused to eat, but the doctor was determined to give them "a dose of their own medicine-man"; two more were hanged before he got the remainder to obey orders and eat. This was a very just retribution, if it can be called punishment for the survivors, for some of them enjoyed the meal! Papuan cannibals do not boil their victims, but skin them and roast the flesh on hot ironstones. It is said that a white man was cooked in his boots, and the cannibals tried to eat them with the body.

Perhaps the voyage of the sloop *Peggy*, described in

the *Annual Register* for 1766, has furnished material for much of the fiction in story and song relating to cannibalism on board ship. On August 27th, 1765, the *Peggy* of New York, with Captain David Harrison, a crew of seven, and a cargo of lumber, pipe-staves, fish, and one negro, sailed for the Azores, where the cargo, with the exception of the negro, who remained unsold, was cleared at Fyal, one of the islands. On October 29th the *Peggy* set sail for New York with a cargo of wine and brandy. She encountered bad weather and could make little way, the ship was leaking, the provisions were exhausted, and it was found necessary in course of time to reduce the daily ration to a small allowance of bread and water. For the Christmas dinner two pigeons were killed, and next day the ship's cat, the sole living creature on board except themselves, shared the same fate. The head fell to the share of the captain, who said he had never in his life tasted anything so delicious. The company then subsisted on barnacles scraped from the ship's bottom, candle-fat, and oil, and the crew regaled themselves with wine.

On January 13th, the crew went to the captain's cabin and told him they could hold out no longer, and must " cast lots which of them should perish for the sustenance of the rest." The captain said he would give no orders on the matter, and they shortly returned to tell him that the lot had fallen on the negro, which was perhaps a foregone conclusion, for the captain said he " had strong suspicions that they had not dealt fairly with the victim." However, the unfortunate creature was dragged to the steerage and shot through the head; a large fire was made, and the body was cut up and cooked; but Campbell, the midshipman, was so ravenous that he seized and ate raw a portion of the liver.

Next day the mate went to the captain and asked for orders as to pickling the remains; the captain was so incensed that he took up a pistol and declared he would send the mate after the negro if he did not retire. The chronicler thought this unreasonable, and remarked that the captain had better have made the same effort to save the poor fellow's life that he now made without necessity. In the result, the crew cut up the body into small pieces and pickled it, throwing overboard the head and hands, thus showing that man as a cannibal acts like the dogs that ate Jezebel and like the man-eating tiger.

It does not appear what the captain subsisted on, but he tells the story, and says he sustained himself with a little dirty water from the bottom of a cask and some drops of "Turlington's balsam." On the third day after the negro's death, Campbell, the midshipman, went mad and died, it was supposed owing to his greediness as already related. They threw the body overboard with some reluctance, fearing to pickle that also owing to the possible consequences of eating it, and they still had some preserved negro. Next day they were preparing their dinner when they said of the captain: "Damn him! though he would not consent to our having any meat, let us give him some;" and immediately one of them went to the cabin and offered him a steak, which he rejected with resentment and menaces. The chronicler remarks that there was not much merit in his abstinence, as he confessed that sickness had taken away his desire to eat.

The meat was finished by January 26th, and on the

29th the crew again approached the captain, said it was better to die separately than all at once, as there was always the hope of rescue, and they must cast lots again. The captain tried to dissuade them, but as they persisted he considered that, if the drawing were managed as before, without him, he might not have fair play, he consented to manage it himself, and he "caused lots to be drawn in the same manner that lottery tickets are drawn at Guildhall." The lot fell on David Flat, a foremast man, and the shock of the decision was so great that the whole company remained silent for a time. The silence was broken by the prospective victim, who thus addressed his mates: "My dear friends and fellow-sufferers, all I have to beg of you is to despatch me as soon as you did the negro, and put me to as little torture as possible." He begged for a short time to prepare himself for death, and his companions agreed. During the interval they lulled their horror with draughts of wine, and prepared for the execution, a fire being kindled in the steerage.

But Flat was greatly respected; they determined that he should live at least until eleven o'clock next morning, and begged the captain to read prayers. The captain then lay down exhausted, and could hear them talking to Flat with earnestness and affection, assuring him they would put out the hooks again on the chance of catching a fish. But by four o'clock in the morning he went raving mad, and later two of the crew came to the captain, and "seizing both his hands fixed their eyes upon him without saying a syllable." Obviously he was to be the victim, for they feared the infection of madness if they ate Flat; so the captain snatched up a pistol and stood upon his defence. They then told him that their behaviour was due to joy at having seen a sail. And so at length they were rescued by the *Susannah* of London, in the Virginia trade, commanded by Captain Thomas Evans, and returning to to London. They reached Land's End on March 2nd, and Captain Harrison went by land to London. Three of the crew, including Flat, survived the voyage, and the chronicle says: "Captain Harrison made the proper attestation of the facts upon oath, and the whole is so authenticated that it would be folly to doubt of its truth."

It is perhaps fitting that man-eating apes, being descended from the same stock as their victims, should be classed as cannibals. Monkeys have been seen to seize a hare, tear it to pieces, and devour it. Chimpanzees in Africa catch and eat fish, in the same way that we used to catch trout when we were boys, thrusting the arm into likely holes in the banks of the stream. Although such instances are rare, there are records of human beings attacked and in some cases killed by apes, and of the occurrence of a man-eating ape in West Africa.

CHAPTER IV

THE LION

ATTEMPTS have been made to depose the King of Beasts, but these are never likely to succeed. The lion, with the majestic appearance imparted by his mane and mien, his place in history, in story, and in heraldry, his mythical character as the type of all that is noble, courageous, and generous, occupies a position in the popular mind of all countries from which he is unlikely to be displaced. He is indeed a noble-looking beast, although, according to Selous, " the lion when roaming by daylight does not carry his head so high as to entitle him to the epithet majestic." But he remains the emblem of valour as the tiger is regarded as the embodiment of ruthless cruelty.

Richard I was " lion-hearted," and many warriors have been " as brave as a lion " ; the Abyssinian Emperor bears the Lion of Judah ; even in India, where the lion is of less account, Ranjit Singh, " the Lion of the Punjab," ruled over the warlike Sikhs, whose independence departed when his strong hand was removed by death ; but in the South of India, Tipu Sultan, regarded as cruel and rapacious, was " the Tiger of Mysore." The lion has the prestige of biblical record, but the tiger is not mentioned in the Bible. Many countries have the lion engraved on their coinage and figured on their standards. But lions as well as tigers appeared in the bloody scenes of the Colosseum when the Roman Emperors staged their triumphs over half-armed barbarians. The lion spared Daniel, was gentle with Una, and grateful to Androcles ; but Ignatius o Antioch, martyred by Trajan, was delivered to lions rather than to tigers.

The lion was better known than the tiger to the ancient world. Not only in North Africa, but in Western Asia and in Southern Europe he was a common object of the country-side. In Rome Pompey exhibited 600 lions at once. The tiger in ancient times inhabited lesser-known parts of the world, and was therefore more rarely brought to Europe. He is supposed to be a comparatively recent immigrant into India and other sub-tropical regions. At one time the lion inhabited a great part of India, but he is now confined to a small corner of that country. It seems possible that he has given way to the stronger animal, for the two beasts are not found in the same locality. It is not implied that the tiger has ejected the lion by force, but that the activities of the invader from Northern Asia may have obliged him to retreat westwards in search of haunts where he would not suffer in the struggle for existence with a beast possessing higher powers of survival.

In Africa the lion is not generally a forest-loving animal, but that is no doubt because his prey is there found in more open country, whereas in India there is more game dwelling in heavy jungle. He may well have been forced from forest regions where the tiger finds his prey, and driven to roam the plains of Western India where he was more liable to molestation by man.

The lion has not attempted to invade the tundras of Northern Asia, which is the supposed cradle of the race of tigers; perhaps the tiger would have repelled such intrusion. It would be an interesting experiment to introduce the tiger into Africa and see whether he would oust the lion from some of his haunts.

No doubt lions, like tigers, possess individual characteristics, making it unwise to generalize from particular specimens. Both animals are courageous, and will often fight when wounded; both are horrible and ferocious when they take to man-eating, but they might stigmatize man in the same way when he takes to lion- and tiger-hunting. "The slothful man saith, 'There is a lion in the way'"; but these great beasts will get out of the way as soon as possible, although a noted naturalist who has travelled much in Africa and has photographed many wild beasts, but, with admirable humanity, killed none, tells me that now the lion has been so persecuted by man that, instead of avoiding him, he will charge his enemy at sight. And who can blame him! Sir A. Pease, one of the most experienced in the ways of the lion, considers it the most valiant of animals—"the mere bravery of the bravest man is matched by the bravery of brutes."

Quot homines, tot sententiae. Selous, great hunter, accurate naturalist and observer, and valiant soldier, who killed 200 lions, termed it the most dangerous animal in Africa. Kittenberger[1] says that in districts where the lion is not often hunted, it will never attack or turn on one, even when wounded. W. D. M. Bell states that among 40 sportsmen who hunted lions seriously in Kenya in one year, 20 were injured and 10

[1] *Big Game Hunting in East Africa.* Edward Arnold.

died of their wounds. An experienced African hunter wrote that he could never understand why the lion was called the King of Beasts, " for on his native soil he is invariably emaciated, frequently mangy, and always crafty." Another characterized it as the most cowardly as well as one of the most astute of animals; and added that " when the lion is wounded it is possible to come close up to him in heavy jungle without his thinking of charging; the only time he summons up courage to charge is when he is cornered." A rat will charge in such circumstances! The man-eaters of Tsavo certainly possessed no kingly qualities, nor did those turned loose in the Roman amphitheatre to devour Christians unless we liken them to the emperors who employed them; and astuteness is an attribute of politicians rather than of kings.

In size there does not appear to be much to choose between the lion and the tiger, but the tiger is supposed to be the heavier of the two, although Sir Samuel Baker expressed the contrary opinion. A comparison of skulls, of weights up to 600 pounds, and length ranging up to 10 feet, indicates that the two animals are much the same in size. In beauty of coloration the tiger is certainly superior, although he lacks the lion's mane, but I have shot tigers with a 3-inch mane on the back of the neck and a splendid ruff round the head. The lion with flowing mane depicted by artists is seldom seen outside a cage, for the mane suffers from wear and tear of thorns and bush, and a well-developed one is seldom seen in a wild beast.

The dull colour of the lion is infinitely inferior to the golden, black and white of the " tiger burning bright in the forests of the night." Indeed, there seems little point in the fable of the ass in the lion's skin, for that despised beast possesses one already, and in the dusk, at any rate, the animals might be mistaken for one another. The ass had little need of disguise; even his tail resembles that of a lion, though the latter may have a thorn concealed in the tuft. A hunter riding through a herd of kongoni, as he thought, suddenly discovered that the supposed antelope were lions.

The lion is a noisy animal, and much has been written about his roar. The tiger is seldom heard, and he would not be so foolish as to warn his prospective prey by roaring about the country. But he has a fine roar on occasion, whereas the lion, if he has not the bray as well as the skin of an ass (and Balaam's ass spoke wisdom!), has at times the note of a bird; he may not, like Bottom, "roar as gently as any sucking dove," but Livingstone said that a European cannot distinguish between the voice of a lion and that of an ostrich. However, we must not be unfair to the lion. He apparently has two voices; so has the tiger, who sometimes cries like a deer. Inverarity, a fine sportsman and observant naturalist, said that in Somaliland lions as they walk about at night keep up a constant singing kind of noise, difficult to describe. It can be heard afar off, and he listened to the lions night after night for hours speaking as they went along. "Some nights they do not talk at all, although their tracks show that they are still about." On this point Selous tells us that lions hunt in silence, and that "lions began to roar loudly, a pretty good sign that they had already dined and were not hunting."

But the lion's roar is undoubtedly, as Sir Alfred Pease says, "heard near at hand, in the dark or in the daylight, a truly terrible and earth-shaking sound. The awful notice to every living beast that their king is walking the silent night to deal out death, whilst it strikes with terror on the ear of every creature of the forest and wilderness, cannot fail to impress the listening man with awe and often with dread." This experienced hunter tells us that "the roar proper consists of an ascending scale of half a dozen awfully deep and loud reverberating roars, ending either with a sigh that makes the air quiver, or low rumbling growls which shake the earth."

The lion charges with the same coughing roar that the tiger does, coming at speed close along the ground, like the tiger and leopard, not springing in the air as is so often described and depicted. The ears are laid back close to the head, the tail, as with the tiger, held stiff and erect. Roosevelt describes the charge of a lion who came towards him "with the speed of a greyhound"; "he came on steadily, ears laid back and uttering coughing grunts." This would describe also the charge of a tiger or a leopard, if not so disabled as to slacken its pace.

A charging lion or tiger is not easy to stop. Sir A. Pease notes a shot that "struck the lion full on the nose, breaking the teeth, cutting along the roof of the mouth, and lodging in the base of the skull. This had no effect on the fury and vigour of the charge." I have experienced the same with a tiger, hit full on the nose, but continuing progress until killed by another bullet; while a tigress, shot in the mouth with a 440-grain bullet from a .500 express rifle, the projectile lodging in the back of the throat, was so lively that she charged fiercely up-hill, and was rolled over at very close quarters. On level ground the charge would have been made good. Mr. George Grey, who was fatally mauled by a lion in 1911, shot the beast in the mouth without checking or turning the charge. But he was using a ·280 Ross copper-pointed bullet, which has velocity and penetration but not the knock-down effect of a projectile with a large striking surface.

The man seized by a lion or tiger is generally knocked flat by the weight and impetus of the beast. His feelings, perhaps, vary according to temperament. Livingstone wrote: "Growling horribly in my ear, he shook me as a terrier does a rat. The shock produced a stupor, similar to that which seems to be felt by a mouse after the first shake of the cat. It caused a sort of dreaminess in which there was no sense of pain or feeling of terror, though quite conscious of all that was happening. It was like what patients partially under the influence of chloroform describe, who see all the operations but feel not the knife. This singular condition was not the result of any mental process. The shake annihilated fear, and allowed no sense of horror in looking round at the beast."

Inverarity, mauled by a lion in Somaliland, says that he felt none of the dreamy stupor described by Livingstone; but, "on the contrary, felt as usual." He lay still, which is the best thing to do, as the animal grabs at everything that moves. He adds that "the claws and teeth entering the flesh do not hurt as much as you would think. The only really painful part of the business is the squeeze given by the jaws on the bone." Tigers and leopards usually leave immediately anyone thus seized in the charge, inflicting a bite or two and not stopping to worry the enemy; in this instance the lioness, having left him, went a few yards to roar at the men, then returned, stood on him growling, and bit his arm.

A leopard is a lighter animal, but my own experience when mauled by one was not pleasant, like that of Dr. Livingstone, nor did I " feel as usual," like Mr. Inverarity. The leopard rushed with a hoarse roar from cover ten yards off, growling fiercely. She made for a Sikh trooper a few paces to my left, but her eyes caught the movement as I raised my rifle, and she turned on me, receiving two ineffectual shots, and seized the left forearm; there was an odour of foul breath in my face, and I was borne violently to the ground, striking the back of my head and being for a moment stunned. My leg was clawed, and the thigh bitten nearly to the bone. There was a confused sound of roars and guns, my companion firing and the trooper beating the beast over the head with the butt-end of my shot-gun, and then the leopard slunk off, pausing to look round as though contemplating a renewal of the fight. One bullet grazed her chest, the other missed. A charge of buckshot would probably have stopped her; she was a big leopard, and as my weight was only about nine stone, owing to illness, she was much heavier.

Lions in Asia are the same as African lions, not maneless as was at one time supposed. They were formerly numerous in Hariana, but had disappeared by 1830. There were lions in Guzerat and Central India, and Babar, the founder of the Moghul Empire, hunted them on the banks of the Indus. In India they are now confined to the Gir Forest, in a corner of the State of Junagadh. The lion appears to have almost disappeared from Persia, the Land of the Lion and the Sun, and from Mesopotamia, where it was at one time plentiful. Layard stated in his *Nineveh* that it was frequently met with on the banks of the Tigris below Bagdad, rarely above. On the Euphrates it has been seen almost as high as Bir, where the steamers of Colonel Chesney's Euphrates Expedition were launched. In the Singar, on the banks of the Khabour, they were frequently caught by the Arabs. They abounded in Khazistan, the ancient Susiana, where Layard often saw three or four together and hunted them with the chiefs of the tribes inhabiting that province. In 1890 Colonel E. B. Burton saw an Arabian lion chained up at the Sultan's gate at Muscat. In 1897 he was told that there were lions in the reed beds where the Mema river exits from Persian Pusht i Kuh into the Tigris Plain, west of Dizful. By 1904 they were almost extinct in Persia, but he saw tracks of a lioness and cub in the sand on the bank of the Karkhah river, near the mounds of Susa, and of another outside a cane brake between Fellahieh and the Karun river, on the road to Muhammarah.

Do lions and tigers ever inhabit the same region, where they would come into contact with one another? Stray lions have been found in Central Indian tiger jungles. Hyrcania was in ancient times famous for tigers, and they still linger along the wooded Elburz chain of mountains which skirts the southern shores of the Caspian. Colonel Chesney noted their occurrence in Daghestan, west of the Caspian, and in Turkish Georgia. Even the borders of Ararat were at one time infested by tigers.

Attempts to separate the lion into local races are as futile as in the case of the tiger. In a recent work on natural history the lion is divided into seven races, each with three Latin names, the distinctions being based on colour and the growth of the mane. Selous says it is doubtful whether any naturalist can refer an assortment of lion skins, selected promiscuously, to their so-called local races. Lions of different colour, with yellow manes or black manes, or no manes at all, are found in one district and even in one family. Out of fifty lions scarcely two will be found alike in colour and length of mane.

While the natural prey of lions abounds in their habitat, they prey also on domesticated animals and on man. They will at times eat carrion, but they prefer to kill their own game. They appear to be even more nocturnal than tigers; Selous says that he only once found a lion hunting by daylight, though they perhaps vary their habits according to locality and climate. Inverarity said that in Somaliland they generally kill in the daytime, the reason being that flocks and herds are secured in a zariba at night. All the natural kills he heard of were in the daytime, though animals tied up as bait were killed at night. They would leap over the high thorn hedges within which the Somalis encamp, and kill and eat their prey on the spot, being unable to leap out again with the animal. He heard of a lion jumping into a zariba and killing and eating a man.

In East Africa lions prefer zebra to other game, but will eat any animal. They are as fond of porcupine as are tigers and leopards; Inverarity observed that they eat quills, paws, and all. Selous mentions a lion killing 100 pigs in a night, and Pease knew of one killing 50 ostriches. The prey is generally seized by the throat, and buffaloes may be heard bellowing when mauled to death by lions. I recollect the bellowing of a buffalo killed in the night by a pair of tigers which I shot next day. A lion has been known to kill an elephant; as they are met with in packs up to 30 or even 40, they could no doubt tackle any large beast. The tiger is comparatively a solitary animal, there being seldom more than two or three in company, and those of one family. But they have been known to kill elephants in Assam and in Burma such kills are not uncommon. Both animals generally begin eating at the hind-quarters. The lion adapts itself to the dry conditions of Somaliland, and is not as impatient of thirst as the tiger, which never wanders very far from water. Lions drink regularly in the hills where there is water, but are able to go for months without, the blood of their prey no doubt supplying its place. They have been shot 30 miles from any water, and they wander over tracts that are waterless for many months.

It is curious that the method of hunting by the great carnivora, whether by scent, sight, or hearing, or a combination of all three senses perhaps in differing degrees, has been generally neglected, and almost ignored in books on sport and natural history. The late F. C. Selous, in his *African Nature Notes and Reminiscences*, wrote that well-known naturalists appear to assume that both carnivorous and herbivorous animals trust entirely to their sense of sight, the former to find their prey and the latter to avoid the approach of their enemies; and he added that "nothing is more certain than that all carnivorous animals hunt almost entirely by scent." Describing the lion's method of hunting, he tells us that "they seek their prey by scent, either smelling the animals directly or following their tracks," while he also says that the leopard hunts by night and by scent.

I drew attention to this matter in a letter to *The Times* of June 22nd, 1928, observing that tigers and leopards in India appear to hunt almost entirely by sight and sound, and seem to have very limited powers of scent. This view was supported by many Indian sportsmen, but the eminent African hunter and naturalist, Mr. Abel Chapman, pointed out that scent, being wind-borne, cannot travel a single yard up wind, and that the many instances adduced, mainly by observers of animal life in India, made no reference to wind when such observers stated that they had been close to tigers without their presence being detected by the animal. Another point he made was that there was confusion in the widely different interpretations of " hunting by scent," his view being that " the lion does not go nosing about the ground, sniffing at the spoor of antelope and other game. He seeks his scent breast-high on the breeze, and instantly detects the position of the game while yet several hundred yards away."

These views were supported by Sir Alfred Pease, who wrote that the *felidae* have not a " hound nose " but a " winding nose," and added that " lions and leopards certainly go up wind to game, kills, and carcasses." He remarks that where lions and leopards show indifference to the presence of man, " even when the wind is from you to them," it must be remembered that lions are usually familiar with the smell of man and will lie close and squat so long as they think they can avoid observation. I have observed this in the case of leopards in India. It is a characteristic of all wild creatures. He instances his following two lions up wind, and running round and ahead of them to get a better shot, and though they both saw him and had his wind, they came on without altering their pace or direction. He adds : " To argue that they had no nose is no better than to argue that they had no sight or hearing, for one came on after I had fired at the other." I would certainly not attempt to dispute such authoritative pronouncements with regard to African animals, especially in the absence of personal knowledge.

The indifference of lions to the presence of man is indicated in an incident related by Colonel H. D. Olivier, who was in Somaliland lying on the ground in a zariba only 3 feet high, close to a lion's kill. A lion came to the kill in daylight and stood looking at it about 25 yards off. Then Olivier heard a deep breath just above his head, and saw the yellow side of another lion approaching from his rear. This lion came and lay down at the kill just 3 feet from his feet. He raised himself slightly and shot No. 1 dead over the back of No. 2, who rushed off but came back when it was quite dark and was also killed. Perhaps the smell of dinner obliterated the smell of man !

It may be added that Mr. Norman Smith, who has wide experience of African hunting, observes that in approaching game up wind, the lion merely does what we ourselves do so that the game should not get our scent. He does not deny to the lion some power of scent, but considers that the felines possess it in a lesser degree than canines, and use it little in hunting.

The views of Professor G. M. Robertson, of the University of Edinburgh, may be added, to the effect that, " speaking generally, animals with a flattened face like that of a cat or of man himself function mainly through their sense of sight. On the other hand, animals with an elongated face, affording accommodation for a large expanse of nasal mucous membrane, rely usually on the evidence of the sense of smell, as, for example, dogs, deer, and horses "—and, it may be added, bears.

Mr. Chapman, in a letter he wrote to me shortly before his death, suggested that as lions live in more open country than do tigers, as for example on the Athi Plains, with no obstructions to scent, probably that would be the chief or only sense employed in hunting; whereas in the thick bush or Indian jungle, scent would be continually deflected or arrested altogether. However, the question so far as it relates to tigers may be dealt with in the chapters concerning those animals.

CHAPTER V

LION-HUNTING

ANCIENT sculptures show lions being speared or shot with bows and arrows, by hunters on foot, in chariots, and on horseback. They are depicted in the sculptures of Nakht i Rustam and Chal Minar (Persepolis), and in Babylon and other places. The lion is not represented in the Assyrian, as in the Egyptian sculptures, tamed and following the king or trained to the chase. Times do not greatly change, except that weapons become more deadly. Lions in our own time have been hunted by men on foot, on horseback, on elephants, and in motor-cars. They have been shot not only with rifles, but with bows and arrows in an expedition organized by an enterprising American sportsman who perhaps got the idea from a bas-relief of an Egyptian king hunting the lion in this manner, and of a lioness dying with three arrows sticking in her body, figured in Sir Alfred Pease's *Book of the Lion*. They have also been speared by the natives of Africa. Then Buffalo Jones and a party of American cowboys brought their horses with them and lassoed a lion and other animals. There is nothing new under the sun ; the Gauchos of the pampas in South America lasso pumas, which are there called lions, using the bolas instead of the looped rope.

The lion is generally found in country very different

from that inhabited by the tiger, and the methods of hunting the two animals therefore naturally vary with the circumstances of their environment and habits. But in Africa and in Asia lions inhabit a variety of country. In North Africa, where, however, they are no longer found, or survive only in small numbers in remote and inaccessible spots, the French hunter Gérard shot them in forests and valleys and wooded hills, where they were confined to a narrow region cut off from southern latitudes by extensive deserts. Perhaps they were at no time numerous in that part of the Continent, for in nine or ten years Gérard killed only 30 lions. Elsewhere they prefer the more open plains with more or less vegetation, where they find their prey. Antelope and zebra, and other animals on which the lion principally preys, as well as domesticated flocks and herds, are found not in dense forest but in open country. When the Uganda Railway was first opened, lions swarmed on the Athi and Kapiti Plains, a vast, rolling, grassy expanse, without trees, and their daily lie-ups or places of siesta were in bush-clad dongas, or amid dense jungle on the few rivers, or in rocky kopjes. There was a well-known bed of huge rushes at mile-peg 300 which, says Mr. Abel Chapman, used to be full of them. They found the railway attractive, perhaps because it afforded a clear and unobstructed pathway, for all animals like paths to walk on.

The late Mr. Inverarity described[1] Somaliland for 30 miles after the traveller leaves the coast at Berbera as a desert, in parts flat, thinly covered with mimosa bush, and in parts rugged sandstone hills almost devoid of vegetation. Here and there a river-bed, for the most

[1] In the *Journal of the Bombay Natural History Society*.

part waterless, affords along its banks for a 100 yards on either side thick cover of thorny bush. In this tract an occasional lion will be found in the dense bush by the river-beds. After 30 or 40 miles there is a range of hills called the Golis, nearly 6000 feet high at the highest point. But there is nothing like this to climb from the foot of the range, for all the way from Berbera the ground has been rising. The hills are steep and stony, and covered with thick bush chiefly of a thorny kind. They are broken up by deep ravines. Lions, elephants, and other animals inhabit these hills. The northern side of the range is very precipitous, the southern slope is a comparatively easy descent, and beyond that the traveller emerges on to an extensive plain about 2000 to 3000 feet above the level of the sea. This is good ground for tracking. It bears umbrella mimosa trees, which grow up 8 or 10 feet to where they form a level table-top 20 feet or more across, and there are dense clumps of thorny bush which afford safe retreats for lions. These clumps are thickly scattered in open sandy ground, thinly covered with thorn bush. The pleateau extends for about 200 miles, and is a fine region for lion-hunting.

Inverarity termed hunting lions in Somaliland "a fascinating pursuit if carried out in the proper manner, which is to track the animal until you come up to where he is lying." At the end of the track, perhaps after many hours, the lion is suddenly seen sitting in the dense gloom of a bush a few feet off, or sometimes the track leads into an impenetrable thorn thicket, which can be fired while the tracker stands to await its egress at the other end. He only once found a lion sitting in the open, under a small tree. This was a lioness with a cub, and so wonderfully did their colour harmonize with the surroundings that they were seen only at four yards' distance, and then only because they got up. On another occasion the men pointed to a lioness crouching in the grass a few yards off, but he could not see her until she moved her ears.

Even so large an animal as a bison in the Indian forest is often betrayed merely by the twitching of its ears as they are flapped to keep off the flies. These considerations may lead one to examine the use of protective coloration, the theory of which has often been carried to excess. Both man and other animals find a difficulty in making out an object which assimilates well with its surroundings until it moves, when it is at once betrayed to a quick eye. Protective coloration is, therefore, of little or no use to an animal in motion, though useful when it is at rest. This is markedly noticeable in the desert-born. In Baluchistan, and in Africa, the birds and the animals in sandy regions take on the dust-coloured hue of their environment. A flock of sandgrouse, so clearly seen when the birds are alighting, disappear like magic when they come to rest on the ground. A gazelle, a bustard, a desert-lark, or a lion is similarly obliterated when at rest, and most difficult to find again if the eyes are taken off it for a moment. A herd of giraffes among the red mimosa start into life and sight only when they move. The lion, the tiger, and the leopard appear like grey shadows in the dusk of night.

Tracking lions is better than beating, the method that has to be generally adopted for tiger-shooting in India, for it makes certain of a shot at close quarters if tracks have been found early enough in the day.

Like all animals, the lion tries to avoid man until wounded, and seldom charges unless it has young ones to guard, or, as Inverarity says, " in astonishment at seeing one so close to them." The same may be said of the tiger, which will, however, sometimes charge, but often not charge home, when it is disturbed at close quarters at its kill.

The other method of hunting lions in Somaliland is to sit up over a kill, but is preferably adopted only in the hills where tracking is impossible. There can be no doubt, however, that this is the method by which most lions are shot in all parts of Africa. A natural kill is best, and as there are no trees, which one generally finds in tiger-country, the plan is to sit on the ground in a zariba or enclosure made of thorns. It should be remembered that a lion can jump over a 12-foot zariba. The enclosure should be about 8 feet in diameter, and have a hole to shoot through ; or one can have a hole cut in a bush and sit in it with a screen of thorns in front. Dark nights are best, for lions are then oftener on the move, and one should sit almost touching the kill. The carcass should be pegged down so that it will not be dragged away by hyenas.

Descriptions of the adventures of the older hunters are always interesting. They found game more plentiful, but they shot with inferior weapons, very different from our modern high velocity rifles. Their ideas on natural history were often inaccurate, but the cult of close observation is a comparatively recent growth. Gordon Cumming did most of his shooting on horseback, and used to hunt lions with a pack of dogs. He describes a typical hunt after a lion seen by his men at the carcass of a buffalo which he had shot the evening before. He started for the place in the morning, and as he and his men appeared he saw the lion, which slunk off, when he slipped his dogs and galloped after it. The lion came to bay in a patch of reeds on the river-bank, where three dogs were killed before he could come up. He then dismounted and fired several shots into the cover where he could hear but could not see the lion. He started pelting it with sticks and earth. After ten minutes of this, the animal made a rush to escape, but the dogs gave chase and brought it to bay in another patch. Again the lion bolted, and made a rush at the pack, and Gordon Cumming got a shot, on receiving which the lion charged growling after the dogs, but only to the edge of the reeds. Cumming now shot it in the head, and it plunged into the river, dyeing the water with blood, and followed by the dogs and a crocodile which was attracted by the blood. The lion swam across, and as it planted its forefeet on the bank it was shot dead.

But lions even in early days when they had been little hunted were not always dealt with so easily, as Mr. C. J. Anderson related in his *Lake Ngami ; Four Years' Wanderings in the Wilds of South-west Africa.* He wounded a lion which put up a good fight, charging twice ; he only escaped by the lion jumping right over him in its second rush. In this case there were no dogs to distract the beast's attention. The best mode of hunting on horseback is no doubt that described by Sir Alfred Pease, where the animal is ridden down, the hunter, however, not riding directly at the lion but keeping at a respectful distance and taking his shot from horseback. Thus, keeping at a distance of 50 or

60 yards, he is able to avoid a charge, and manœuvre as may be necessary.

While numerous books have been written about lion-hunting in Africa, there is little recorded about the Asiatic animal. There are, however, some articles on the subject in several defunct Indian periodicals, and Colonel L. S. Fenton contributed to the Bombay Natural History Society's Journal an interesting account of his experiences with this animal. The Gir Forest, where alone the lion in India now survives, occupies an area of some 1500 square miles in the State of Junagadh. The greater part is covered with dwarf teak, acacia, and other stunted trees, containing also patches of bamboo, corinda, and other thorny bushes, and an occasional banyan tree towering above the others. The undulating ground is cut up by water-courses with rocky beds and a thick growth upon their banks, and there are a few rugged hills. The only river is the Thram which, as well as some of the larger nullahs, contains pools of water. The few villages consist of dilapidated huts surrounded by patches of cultivation. The leopard and hyena share this forest with the lion, but there are no tigers. Game includes nilgai, pig, Indian antelope, and gazelle, while there is an abundance of cattle, among which lions do an enormous amount of damage.

The old idea that Asiatic lions are maneless has long been exploded. They have as good manes as those of Africa, from which they do not differ in size or in any other respect. The average length is about 9 feet, the same as that of the tiger; Lord Harris shot one 9 feet 7 inches long; the largest measured by Colonel Fenton was 9 feet 5 inches. There are black-maned lions in

India as in Africa. The habits of the animal are the same as in Africa; the Gir Forest lions are addicted to roaring at night, thus facilitating the finding of their tracks in the morning. They cover a great deal of ground in their nightly wanderings, and they lie up in the shade of a tree or in a waterhole. They are usually beaten out and shot, or walked up by the sportsman, the latter being the best way to make sure of a shot, and some have been bagged by what Colonel Fenton calls "the ignominious way" of sitting up over a goat. He shot one of two lions which during the previous night broke into a cattle-zariba, killed three cows, and mauled two more. A sixth was missing, but was found grazing near the lions where they lay fast asleep two miles away, "having evidently been driven by them to serve for their next meal." Like tigers, lions vary in character and temperament. Some of Colonel Fenton's lions charged, and others did their best to get away even when wounded.

An unhappy accident happened in 1905 when Lord Lamington, Governor of Bombay, went to the Gir with a party which included Major Carnegy, the Political Officer. A lion was wounded, and was being followed up when it charged, and Major Carnegy was killed. That is the sole recorded fatality to an Englishman in hunting lions in Kathiawar.

Lions were at one time plentiful not only in Guzerat but in Hariana, from whence they disappeared over a hundred years ago. In the sixteenth century the Emperor Babar, founder of the Moghul Empire, not only hunted the rhinoceros on the banks of the Indus, as described in his entertaining Memoirs, but killed lions, buffaloes, and elephants in the neighbourhood of

Benares. It is curious that, thirty years after the last lion was killed in Hariana, no traditions of the animal remained in that part of the country. It was still found in Guzerat in 1857, and it extended into the Saugor and Narbada territories. In 1847 one was killed in the Damoh district by a native hunter; in 1850 two were seen near Goona. In 1865 a party of officers stationed at Morar in Gwalior, as described in the *Oriental Magazine* for 1871, found three lions and killed two twelve miles west of that place. No lions had been seen near Gwalior for twenty years, although they were still pretty plentiful about seventy miles to the south.

In 1866 a party of three, engaged in the construction of the Jubbulpore railway, killed a lion a short distance to the west of the eightieth mile from Allahabad near the village of Putna in the Raj of Pattacachar. They had expected a tiger in the beat, and "were astonished to see a fine lion striding towards them with a majestic air"; it was killed without difficulty. The natives were equally astonished, having never before seen such an animal. The lion was 8 feet 3 inches in length, and 3 feet 3 inches in height at the shoulder, with a girth of 3 feet 10 inches round the chest. He had a fair mane, with hair 11 inches in length, a large tuft of hair behind each foreleg at the elbow, and his skin was as sleek as that of a healthy greyhound; his tail had a fine tuft of black hair at the tip. General Travers and Colonel Cunliffe Martin shot two lions west of Goona in 1860, and in 1862 Colonels Martin and Beadon killed eight near Patalgarh, seventy miles north-west of Goona. The late Sir Montague Gerard told me that in June 1872 he shot the last lion killed in Central India, nine miles from Goona; but Hughes-Buller of the Central India Horse saw one in Gwalior State in 1884.

A correspondent of the *India Sporting Review*, who had shot lions in Hariana, wrote that " they did not always show fight, but generally slunk away ; when they did fight, they took to an open plain ; it was difficult to get an elephant to face them, and few would stand a charge. When a lion charges, his mane and tail are erect." The following account of a Hariana lion was given in the *Bengal Sporting Magazine* for 1833 : " He had just dined off a fine buffalo, and we had put him out of a small bush of jungle close to the scene of his repast, when he sneaked off behind us without a shot, as we were afraid of hurting the sowars (troopers). We were soon informed that he was in the plain waiting for us ; and immediately on our coming out from the jungle, and while we were 100 yards from him, down he came lashing his sides with his tail, his mane erect, and roaring dreadfully. Everyone of the elephants took to their heels, whereupon the lion returned to his position, which was a high knoll from which he overlooked us, but which also rendered him conspicuous and was the cause of his death at last. The elephants were frequently brought back to the charge, and as often driven away in a similar manner ; and we were obliged to have recourse to the unsportsmanlike plan of picking him off from a distance, which we were able to do from the raised and open position he had taken up."

An account of another lion-hunt was given in his *Pen and Pencil Sketches* by Captain Mundy. A wounded lion charged fearlessly at the elephant on which was the hunter who had shot it ; the latter leaned over the front of the howdah and took aim, but the whole front gave way with a crash and he was precipitated on to the lion, which at once seized him. His companions could not shoot for fear of hitting him. But the mahout brought up the elephant, which grasped the top of a tree and bent it down across the loins of the lion, forcing it to quit hold of its victim. The latter was terribly mauled, but his life was saved, and the lion was disposed of.

Lions were formerly plentiful in the Bakhtiari mountains, where to kill a lion, especially in single combat, was considered a great feat. The figure of a lion carved in stone is placed by the Bakhtiari over the graves of their warriors to denote that they were men of valour. Layard, in his *Early Adventures*, relates that he went after a lion with Mehemet Taki Khan, a Bakhtiari Chief. One of the men wounded the animal, which pulled down another man. The Chief dismounted, and, advancing towards the beast, addressed it thus in a loud voice : "O lion ! these are not fit antagonists for thee. If thou desirest to meet an enemy worthy of thee, contend with me !" The lion was not disposed to abandon its victim, whom it was holding down under its massive paws. It raised its head majestically as if defying its numerous foes. The Chief approached it, and drawing a long pistol from his girdle, shot it in the head. It was then quickly despatched by the guns, swords, and spears of his followers. It had a short black mane. The great Chief's valour remained a tradition among the tribes.

CHAPTER VI

MAN-EATING LIONS

THE literature of man-eating lions is somewhat scanty, although the subject attained wide publicity from Colonel Patterson's famous work, *The Man-eaters of Tsavo*, and a few details regarding other man-eaters are scattered in books descriptive of travel and sport in Africa. But there are no records and statistics like those relating to India, which is only to be expected in a continent of vast extent, divided into many States and Governments, and only opened up and provided with rail and road communications within the lifetime of many of us.

Selous found that man-eating lions are almost invariably worn-out animals, and that "in the vast majority of cases a lion only takes to human beings in its declining years, and when its strength is failing." This is in accordance with the popular idea, and it is more probable where the natural prey of the animal, whether lion or tiger, is still abundant. The vast herds of antelope and other animals which were seen by early hunters have been enormously reduced. Indeed, Gordon Cumming himself indulged in much butchery, as in the slaughter of giraffes, while the opening up of Africa and the introduction of long-range, high-velocity rifles of extreme accuracy has led to a measure of extermination in some parts. Where the predatory beasts have not been correspondingly reduced, the balance of nature has been upset, and the lions have had to turn to domesticated beasts and even man himself for prey. Perhaps in both Africa and India, when game was more plentiful, man-eaters were generally old or disabled animals, and this may have led to ideas now found to be erroneous, man-eaters being often vigorous and in the prime of life.

A few years ago the Chief Game Warden of Uganda reviewed the occurrence of man-eating lions in that province, where they were especially destructive in the Sanga district of Ankole, between Lake Victoria and the Belgian Congo. He remarked that the reign of terror which existed in recent years on the Mbarara-Masaka road in the vicinity of Sanga was not caused by one lion but by many. The Indian Game Ranger told him that one lion was responsible for 84 deaths, and that another had killed more than 40 human beings before it was destroyed. He expressed a somewhat new theory when he ascribed the propensity, where lions take to man-eating collectively, to a taint in their blood which " is naturally passed on to their offspring, though the new generations may not necessarily display man-killing tendencies from birth. The taint is, however, lying dormant, awaiting an opportunity to display itself."

This question is discussed later on in the chapter dealing with man-eating tigers. It is scarcely probable that the practice is due to a hereditary taint. Acquired characteristics are rarely if ever inherited, and there seems no reason why a taste for human flesh should be thus passed on by lions any more than cannibalism in man. More likely it is a characteristic acquired from a man-eating lioness, and transmitted by feeding the young on human flesh, and by their learning to kill human beings. It may thus be perpetuated.

Both lion and tiger man-eaters often have defective teeth, or suffer some disablement from wounds or deformity, rendering it difficult for them to catch wild game. But in numerous cases man-eaters have no disability. The Chief Game Warden says the Sanga man-eaters were virile animals living in districts where a sudden reduction of other natural prey was due to rinderpest or anti-rinderpest measures. The starving lions took to raiding flocks and herds and so to preying on human beings after tasting human blood. Many lions hunted in troops, sharing the first few human victims; thus they acquired a taste for human flesh and also found man an easy prey. This would lead to widespread transmission of the habit to the young.

One would expect, therefore, to find many more man-eating lions than tigers, which do not hunt or assemble in herds, but at most in small families. Every lion in the Sanga district was considered to be a potential man-eater, and although they might be in a locality well-stocked with game, they preferred to prowl round the labour camps. The Game Warden compares them with the bush lions of Tanganyika, which, he says, are man-eaters from birth, and with the tigers of the Sundarbans of Bengal.

There was a strange story from Gomba, where a herd of elephants was found to be attended by a lion whose tracks were obliterated by their feet. The lion took advantage of the elephant raids on gardens to seize human beings who assembled in the banana clumps, beating drums to drive away the elephants. An apathy similar to that often prevailing in India with regard to the presence of wild beasts was found in some districts, although there is no evidence to show whether it was due to similar superstitions or merely to laziness or indifference. In one case a village was raided by lions, and cattle were carried off, but the Game Ranger was not told for 12 hours, although his camp was only half a mile away. In another instance a man-eating lioness was living in close contact with a village just as Captain Forsyth found wolves, and as I have found leopards in India, where this apparent apathy is due either to Hindu prejudice or to the superstition that the informer will be the next victim of the tiger or leopard.

The lion is more abundant in Africa than is the tiger in India, and it is as much addicted to man-eating. The loss of life must, therefore, be if anything greater in Africa. A few well-known stories relate to European victims in Africa. The earliest is that of Hendrick, one of Gordon Cumming's men, which is of additional interest because it illustrates, like so many other stories, the futility of a camp-fire as in itself a protection against attack, although the fire has its uses in revealing the approach of an animal to the watcher; but the wild beast does not fear the fire.

Gordon Cumming relates that the night was pitch dark and windy when the appalling roar of an angry lion burst upon his ears within a few yards, followed by the shrieking of the Hottentots. He heard two of his men, John Stofolus and Ruyter scream; next instant Stofolus rushed up almost speechless with fear, his eyes bursting from their sockets, and shrieked out: "The lion, the lion! He has got Hendrick; he dragged him away from the fire beside me; I struck him with the burning brands upon his head, but he would not let go his hold. Hendrick is dead! O God! Hendrick is dead! Let us take fire and seek him." The rest of the people rushed up, shrieking as if they were mad, which, says Cumming, "made me angry with them for their folly, and I told them that if they did not keep quiet, the lion would in all probability have another of us." He then ordered the dogs to be let loose, and the fire increased as much as possible. He shouted Hendrick's name, but all was still, and he had everything brought into the kraal and the entrance closed. He adds that "to help the dead man was impossible." In such cases guns or rifles should be fired off at once, and it is not clear why Cumming did not at once head a rush of men and dogs with fire-brands after the lion, which might then have dropped its prey, dead or alive. But, he says, the dogs, instead of going at the lion, rushed at one another and fought desperately for some minutes; after this they got his wind, and going at him showed his position, and kept up a continual barking until day dawned, the lion occasionally driving them in upon the kraal. The monster had dragged his prey into a hollow at the back of a thick bush, and here, within 40 yards of the camp, devoured him.

It appeared that Hendrick had risen to drive in an ox, and he had scarcely lain down when the lion sprang upon him and Ruyter, grappling him with his claws and biting his breast and shoulder, all the while feeling for his neck; having got hold of which he at once dragged him away backwards across the bush into the dense shade. As the animal lay upon him, Hendrick cried : " Help me, help me ! O God, men ! help me." After which all was still except for the cracking of the bones of his neck between the lion's teeth. John Stofolus, who was lying on the other side of the fire, sprang up and, seizing a brand from the burning, beat the beast over the head, but it took no notice of him. Later next day they inspected the scene of the tragedy and found a leg of the man in a hollow where the lion had consumed his prey, the shoe still on the foot; the grass and bushes were all stained with blood. Farther on the brute was brought to bay by the dogs and shot without difficulty.

Cotton Oswell, who hunted in South Africa at the same time as Gordon Cumming, related that some Kaffir women were working in the fields, and a young man was standing on the edge of the bush talking to them, when a lioness seized him and was carrying him off. The man's wife ran after the beast and caught her by the tail and was dragged along for some distance. The lioness slackened her pace and the brave woman straddled her back and hit her across the nose with a heavy short-handled hoe until she dropped her prey and slunk back to cover.

The pluck of natives should not be forgotten. The Masai and other tribes spear lions, and a story is told of one being thus killed by a couple of youths with no other help. Sir Alfred Pease tells of a Somali camel-man who was tending horses when one of them was attacked by a lion. He fought it all alone with his spear and killed it, being himself maimed and bleeding from the combat. Such courage makes a sportsman think little enough of slaying wild beasts with powerful rifles ! Asked if he was not very frightened, he said that he was, but more frightened of what would have been said if he went back and had let the lion kill the horse, and had done nothing. Many natives have laid down their lives for their masters. A Somali with his bare hands pulled a lion off Lord Delamere, seizing it by the head on both sides, and being himself maimed for life. Many similar heroic deeds have been recorded.

The lions of Tsavo speak for themselves in terrible accents in Colonel Patterson's dramatic account of their depredations. They had the distinction of mention in Parliament, when Lord Salisbury, the Prime Minister, said in the House of Lords, when speaking of the construction of the Uganda Railway: "The whole of the works were put a stop to for three weeks because a party of man-eating lions appeared in the locality and conceived a most unfortunate taste for our porters. At last the labourers entirely declined to go on unless they were guarded by an iron entrenchment. Of course it is difficult to work a railway under these conditions, and until we found an enthusiastic sportsman to get rid of these lions, our enterprise was seriously hindered."

The Tsavo man-eaters were fortunately destroyed by Patterson when they had killed no more than twenty-eight of the Indian coolies employed on the railway, but they had also slain some scores of natives. There is seldom any detailed description of such deaths of African natives, or of statistics of the number killed by particular animals. In India, one man-eater, tiger or leopard, has been known to account for as many as 300 victims.

Colonel Patterson's story has a bearing on the question of the value of fire or light as a deterrent from the attacks of wild beasts. He evidently started with the usual assumption that this is in itself a source of safety, for he says with regard to his walking some distance in the dark on the way to his first watch for the man-eaters : " I felt fairly safe as one of my men carried a bright lamp close behind me." Later a lamp afforded no protection to his guest, Mr. Whitehead, who was attacked by a lion when on his way from the station to the camp, and only saved from death by firing off his rifle. The lion then turned on the native who accompanied him, carrying a lamp, killed him, and devoured him so near to the camp that Patterson heard the crunching of his bones.

In the Hindu hymn of praise addressed to Colonel Patterson after he had killed the man-eaters, it was written of the people : ' Every one of them kept a fire burning at night, and none dared to close his eyes in sleep ; yet would some of them be carried away to destruction." In a raid on the hospital a man was dragged out of a tent by the foot, and killed within the circle of light of a big camp-fire.

Perhaps the most tragic and at the same time pathetic story is that of the death of the engineer O'Hara, who was employed on road-making, and, with his wife and two children, was in camp twelve miles from Voi. They were asleep in the tent, with a sentry by the camp-fire not far off, and the tent door was open. Mrs. O'Hara awoke feeling the pillow pulled away from under her head, and missed her husband. She jumped up and called out, but no answer came. She heard a noise at the door, rushed out, and saw her husband lying between the boxes. She called to the sentry to come and help her to lift him, but he refused, saying there was a lion beside her. She looked up and saw the beast glowering at her not more than two yards away. The sentry fired his rifle, and the lion went off. But O'Hara was dead. All four askaris (native soldiers) came, and they placed the corpse on the bed; but the lion came back, and all night continued to prowl round the tent, growling and purring, and did not go until daybreak. It was only kept off by firing rifles at intervals. The poor widow arrived at Voi next day, one child holding on to her skirt, and carrying the baby in her arms; her husband's body was borne on a stretcher by the four men. Colonel Patterson received this pitiful procession at Voi. It is satisfactory to know that the lion was soon afterwards shot by a native with a poisoned arrow.

The story of the man-eater in a railway carriage has often been told, but it cannot be omitted from this volume. On June 6th, 1900, Mr. Ryall, Superintendent of Police, was on inspection duty on the Uganda railway, accompanied by two friends. They arrived at a small station, where news was received that a lion had been seen close by shortly before the arrival of the train. They agreed to remain for the night, in the hope of shooting the beast, which had carried off and eaten a number of the railway staff, and the carriage was shunted on to a siding. There were two sleeping berths in the carriage, one above the other. Ryall lay on the lower one, one of his friends on the upper one, and the other on the floor. After dinner they watched for some time, but as there was no sign of the man-eater, Ryall said he would keep watch, while the other two slept. The door was probably partly open, and was pushed back by the lion, which entered the carriage, when, being on a slope, the door slipped to again, shutting the man-eater inside with the three men. The beast stood on the man on the floor with its paws on Ryall, whom it seized and killed, and then burst its way through the window on one side and made off with its prey. There was a sliding door leading into the other half of the carriage, occupied by the native servants. While the lion had hold of Ryall, the man on the top berth actually jumped on to its back and from there managed to get through into the servants' compartment, a moment before a crash announced the departure of the man-eater. The man on the floor then left by the opposite carriage window and took refuge in the station.

While natives of Uganda are often ready to deal with a troublesome lion by attacking it with spears, in some other parts of Africa they seem to be rather helpless. Mr. R. C. F. Maugham, while travelling in Zambesia, observed a number of deserted villages. He was told that they had been abandoned owing to the depredations of man-eating lions. These animals usually attacked at night, getting on to the roof of a hut and tearing open the thatch, entering before the occupants were awake, or finding them too paralysed with fear to attempt to escape.

A remarkable escape[1] was that of the Transvaal Game Ranger, Mr. Wolhuter, who was riding one evening at sundown, accompanied by a dog, and was about three miles from his destination when a lion seized his horse and unseated him. At that moment a second lion charged, picked up Wolhuter in his jaws, and made off with him, dragging him along the path on his back, and in trotting along trampled on him,

[1] Recorded in the *Journal of the Society for the Protection of Fauna of the Empire.*

lacerating his thighs. He had dropped his rifle, and the lion held his right shoulder and arm. Fortunately he thought of the sheath-knife which was carried in his belt. With difficulty he managed to draw it—a 3-inch steel blade. After dragging him 200 yards, the lion stopped under a tree, and Wolhuter, with fine courage and presence of mind, and the knife in his left hand, stabbed him twice where he judged the heart to be; the lion dropped him at once, and stood growling, and the Ranger then struck the beast in the throat with all his force, severing a large vein, for he was deluged with blood. The lion retreated a few yards, and stood facing him, still growling. Wolhuter scrambled to his feet, expecting a further attack, and then, remembering what he had heard of the power of the human voice, shouted "all the opprobrious epithets he could muster." The lion then went off and was lost to sight in the darkness. But the growls, now turning to moans, could still be heard, until they became fainter and then ceased.

Already, however, he had climbed up the tree, and it was well he did so, for the other lion, having followed his blood, came up with a rush. But now the gallant dog, encouraged by his master, went for the lion, and at length succeeded in putting it to flight. Soon Wolhuter heard the voices of his men, who had been a mile or two behind him on the way, and with their help got down from the tree, and with pain and difficulty made his way to camp. In the morning the horse was found quietly grazing in the bush; the lion was dead. He was an old male, his canines worn quite flat, his stomach empty.

There are several interesting points about this narrative, apart from the remarkable escape of the Ranger, who recovered from his wounds. No man-eaters had been heard of, and it seems probable that men on foot would not have been attacked, the horse being the quarry. Wolhuter was seized, he thought, even before he touched the ground, and perhaps the lion did not know what he had got hold of until he tasted blood. The incident shows, however, that, as man-eating must have a beginning, anyone in the haunts of beasts of prey may meet the beginner. It is noticeable that the lion would not renew the attack when he was faced, a fact which bears out the idea that it is safest to face a wild beast. Had Wolhuter turned to run, he would probably have been seized again. Whether the second lion followed the tracks by scent or by sound is not certain ; he may have used either sense, or both.

It is certainly wise to carry a hunting-knife, or other second weapon for use as a last resort. Captain Shakespear used to buckle a sword round his waist, a somewhat cumbersome weapon, especially in a hot climate where an ounce or two extra weight is oppressive. Some 45 years ago a Major Lyon was being dragged off by a tiger when he shot it with a pistol. He escaped with the loss of a limb. But surely Wolhuter's adventure furnishes the only instance of a lion being killed with a 3-inch knife !

The Asiatic lion is more dangerous to flocks and herds than to men. There are no records of man-eating lions in India, and few in Persia. Sir Oliver St. John was attacked by a lion which sprang on to his horse's hind-quarters, but it was probably after the horse and not the man. Layard, in his *Early Adventures*, gives a few instances of man-eating lions. One of a party of Bakhtiaris with whom he was hunting was missing one morning, and his remains were discovered eaten by a lion near the spot where they had passed the night in the open. Stories of travellers being attacked and devoured formed part of the evening's talk in the Lurs' tents. During three years a lion haunted the plains of Ram Hormuz. Scarcely a night passed without a human being, a horse, or cow being carried off. The animal would enter huts and tents in search of human prey. It was killed when the Governor of Ispahan with his army passed through the plain. In the night the lion carried off a soldier, whose remains were found in a thicket to which it was tracked, and a detachment of the Luristan regiments slew it after it had wounded two men. Layard saw the dead animal; it was unusually large, of a dark brown colour, in some parts of its body approaching to black.

CHAPTER VII

THE TIGER

THE tiger does not ordinarily inhabit what are commonly known as deserts, notwithstanding Bishop Heber's lines :

> Far off, in deserts dank and rude,
> The tiger holds his solitude.

The lines might perhaps apply to tigers inhabiting the swamps and reed-beds, called tundras, of Northern Asia, which are indeed supposed to be the cradle of the race. In many parts of India the tiger affects the neighbourhood of the habitations of man, whose cattle furnish it with food, and whose standing crops attract the deer, antelope, and pig on which it largely sustains life ; but there must be within reach enough cool retreats in extensive forest. At the same time many tigers are to be found inhabiting remote regions far from human haunts, where no sounds but those of Nature strike upon the ear, and where bison and other retiring beasts can wander in peace over almost untrodden solitudes. In such surroundings the game-killing tiger finds his natural prey. With the spread of railways and other means of communication, however, such solitudes tend to become more restricted, more accessible, and more frequently disturbed.

The tiger inhabits a large part of Asia and, although best known in India as an Indian animal, is supposed to be a comparatively recent immigrant into India. Its impatience of heat and the woolliness of the young have been adduced as reasons for this supposition, although in tropical or sub-tropical latitudes all animals alike are susceptible to extreme heat, and many are covered with thick hair, which is thicker in the young in some cases. Some skins of Northern Asia tigers, displayed at the Nijni Novgorod Fair in 1893, were of great size and had long fur. Certainly in the hot weather the tiger avoids the sun as much as possible and is in general a nocturnal animal. When driven from its lair, or when hunting in the heat of the day, the tiger pants with lolling tongue and slavering jaws. But in cold or cool weather he not infrequently seeks his prey by day, as he does in the supposed country of his origin.

It seems probable that the animal migrated into India from the north-east after the separation of Ceylon from the mainland, for it is not found in that island. It has been suggested in the Proceedings of the Zoological Society that "there is reason to think that the users of the Sanscrit language were not acquainted with the animal, as there is no Sanscrit word for tiger." This would place immigration at less than two thousand years ago, when Sanscrit ceased to be a spoken language; but the reason given is not correct, for there is a Sanscrit word *vyaghra* for tiger, as there is *citra-vyaghra* for spotted tiger or leopard. There are also references to tigers in the "Mahabharata." But the advent of the tiger into India may be placed much farther back. There have been dug up at Mohenjo Daro, a buried city in the Indus Valley, some seals on which tigers are figured. On one seal a man is shown sitting in a tree, angrily apostrophizing a tiger which is waiting for him below. This indicates that tigers were known in India at least 5000 years ago, that being the date ascribed to the buried city.

The remains of primordial tigers, perhaps similar to the sabre-toothed tiger of Europe, are found in the Siwalik hills. But whether these animals were more like tigers than lions or leopards is not known. A recent eminent authority on natural history has now grouped all these animals into one genus and given them the generic name of *panthera*. Coloration of existing species seems to indicate that the original ancestors from which the great cats are descended were spotted. Young lions and pumas are spotted; in hybrids between lion and leopard the spotted species predominates; there is no record of tiger-leopard hybrids, but the "tigon," a cross between a tiger and a lioness, now in Regent's Park, presents more of the characteristics of the tiger than of the lion. This is a fine male with a tigrine face; there are no "sun-spots" over the eyes, but the stripes are visible, although the colour is leonine. A hybrid leopard-lioness, bred in the gardens at Kohlapur, was covered with rosettes and was more of a leopard than a lion, indicating the biological predominance of the more primitive type, as would be expected. These facts point to the conclusion that the ancestral type was spotted; that the tiger comes next in order of evolution, its stripes being elongated spots or rosettes, and most tigers having some spots, while lynxes, young lions, and pumas, and many old lions, especially in Somaliland, are spotted. Mature tigers also often exhibit spots. The conclusion is, therefore, that the unicoloured felines, the lions and pumas, come last in order and are the most recent examples of adaptive coloration. Attempts have been made to separate the tiger into local races, distinguished by the character of the stripes ; but no two tigers are striped exactly alike, and no particular form of stripe belongs to any particular locality.

The tiger attains an extreme length of some inches over ten feet, the tail being usually about three feet ; the tigress measures a foot or more less, measurements being taken in a straight line from the nose to the tip of the tail. But the male is much the larger and heavier animal, attaining an extreme weight of 600 pounds, which is, however, greatly above the average ; a tigress weighs from 250 to 300 pounds. Length depends on the manner of measurement. Measured round the curves, they may be nearly a foot more. In old books claims are made of tigers exceeding 12 feet in length. These were probably measured carelessly or from stripped skins. A tiger is a very symmetrical animal, and if one be sketched out on a wall in proper proportion, it will be realized that a 12-foot tiger is an unimaginable monster.

It is generally said that tigresses are more numerous than tigers. This is not my experience, nor would it be expected, as the two cubs that usually survive and accompany a tigress with young are generally, though not always, male and female. My shooting diary records in 1895–99 twenty-six tigers shot to fourteen tigresses in one area of the Deccan. As many as five cubs have been cut out of a dead tigress ; in one case, at any rate, three of these were males ; three or four cubs have been found accompanying a tigress, though this is rare; they remain with her about two years, when they are able to kill their own game and are left to fend for themselves. I once found tracks of a tigress accompanied by two small cubs and a much larger one of an earlier litter.

The age of the tiger has been estimated at about twenty years, which is probably the extreme limit of life in the wild state; but in the unhealthy conditions of captivity they are unlikely to live so long. One old pair, which the natives of a village near which they were shot said they had known for thirteen years, were faded, with broken teeth. The natives have a theory that the age can be determined from the number of lobes in the liver, one for each year, but an examination of many livers has disproved this.

Value for medicinal and other purposes is attached by the natives of India to various products of the tiger. The fat is highly valued, and when a tiger is killed, the flesh is boiled down and the fat carefully bottled as an aphrodisiac and as a remedy for rheumatism. The clavicles or "lucky bones," rudimentary collar-bones found loose in the flesh of the neck, and the claws are prized as charms and ornaments; the whiskers have to be looked after when a tiger is shot, or they will be surreptitiously plucked out, it is said for use as "medicine" for poisoning enemies, just as ground glass is commonly used in India as an irritant poison, perhaps given in a cup of tea. The liver is eaten to impart courage, and the tigress's milk is valued as an application for sore eyes.

Historically the tiger is a most interesting animal. In the Deccan *bagh* or *wagh*, derived from the Sanscrit *vyaghra*, is applied to both tiger and leopard or panther, while the lion is *oontia bagh* to denote its drab coloration, *oont* being camel. The natives in some parts think that a leopard is a young tiger, whence perhaps *borbacha* for leopard. The word for tiger or leopard is preserved in the names of places, such as Waghdo, Wagholi, Waghderi—the place of the tiger; it occurs in waghnak, the terrible Mahrati weapon made of steel claws with which Sivaji, the founder of the Mahratta Empire, killed Afzul Khan, the Moghul general.

Tipu Sultan was commonly called "the Tiger of Mysore," and his admiration of the animal was unlimited. He is credited with saying that it were better to live two years as a tiger than 200 years as a sheep, a historical variant of the excellent advice to "live dangerously." Not only was Tipu's nature comparable with that of the proverbially cruel tiger, but that animal furnished the symbol of his power. His flag was a green square set off with the tiger stripes in the sides and angles; golden tigers were figured on his throne; his cipher was a tiger's face, and in his territory was the Tiger Rock from which prisoners of war were hurled to destruction and the wild beasts. A musical tiger was found in his palace at Seringapatam and sent to the museum of the East India Company in London.

Arthur Wellesley, afterwards Duke of Wellington, was present at the discovery of the Sultan's body under a heap of slain in the gateway where he died, fighting bravely to the last in defence of his capital. Wellesley was made Commandant of Seringapatam after the assault on May 4th, 1799, and on the 5th he wrote to General Harris: "There are some tigers here which I wish Meer Alum (Commander of the Nizam's

Cavalry) would send for, or else I must give orders to have them shot, as there is no food for them, and they are getting violent."

Later, during the settlement of Mysore, Wellesley undertook an arduous and skilfully conducted campaign for the destruction of a large body of marauders who devastated the country under Dhundia Wagh (" Tiger " again !), a Mahratta trooper who was released after the capture of Seringapatam, and took the title of " King of the Two Worlds." He was despatched to the other world in a final encounter when the English general charged at the head of his cavalry. Dhundia did well to call himself *Wagh*, the Tiger, for he carried out a terrible vengeance on his enemy, the Mahratta chief Gokhale, who had attacked and plundered his camp, and dispersed his followers. But Dhundia again gathered strength, and swore to slay his enemy and dye his moustaches in his heart's blood, a vow he literally fulfilled when he surprised and destroyed Gokhale and his attendants.

The tiger is found throughout India in favourable localities where there is sufficient cover, water, and food, but it has been exterminated in some districts, as in the Punjab, where only three tigers were destroyed and two people killed by them in 1878. It extends through Central Asia to the Caucasus, though sparsely distributed in Iraq and Persia, and has now perhaps altogether disappeared from those countries. It is found in the Malay Peninsula, in Burma, in Corea and Northern and Southern China, and in Java and Sumatra. It preys principally on deer, antelope, and wild pig, resorting for food also to domesticated animals and more rarely to man himself. General Briggs, giving evidence before a Parliamentary Committee about seventy years ago, stated that during the four years he was in Khandeish, in Western India, upwards of 350 men and 24,000 head of cattle were devoured by tigers.

When pressed for food the tiger is known to indulge in strange diet. I have observed in the stomach of the animal remains of scorpions and other insects, and have found evidence of their eating snakes, crabs, and fish. They are expecially partial to porcupines, whose quills are often found embedded in their paws and other parts of the body; one great tiger had suppurating wounds and quills in the back of his neck, indicating that he had rolled on a porcupine, although the natives say these animals propel quills at their enemies like arrows from a bow. On one occasion a goat tied up as bait was found dead, pierced through the heart by several quills. Tigers or leopards eat the pangolin or scaly ant-eater; they must find it difficult to get at an animal which rolls itself up in a ball and presents an armour-plated surface that is impervious to the teeth of most beasts. I once found in a pool of water a large python bitten in half and partly eaten by a tiger. Cannibalism is not unknown; the dropping of a large tiger consisted of tiger's hair in which a claw was embedded; the tiger was lame on one hind foot, as evinced by his tracks; he had probably had a fight and devoured his antagonist, sustaining injury in the encounter, but I did not bring him to bag. Tigers also eat bears. I found the remains of two bears, evidently killed and eaten by a tiger, on the top of a hill near Fort Mahor above the Pein Gunga, and a number of similar cases has been recorded, while a she-bear has been seen to rush up and attack a tiger which had just been shot dead in a beat. I have driven tigers, bears, and panthers out of the same cover, in which they appear to have been living amicably, or at least without fighting; probably the lesser animals took good care to keep out of the way of the tiger.

The tiger usually hunts by night, for it is impatient of heat, but I have known one to kill a buffalo in the middle of the day at the hottest season of the year, and they wander more during the cold weather, when water and cover are more abundant. In view of what has been said about the senses used by the lion in hunting, it will be understood that there is room for differences of opinion regarding the tiger. The consensus of opinion expressed in *The Times* correspondence, already referred to, is that the tiger has very limited powers of scent, and hunts almost entirely by sight aided by hearing. Its sight is not of the best, though it is quick to perceive movement, but we may all find it difficult to pick out a stationary object. A tiger will stare for some time with unseeing eyes at an object at short range, unable to make it out until it is betrayed by movement, when the tiger sees it in an instant. As to scent, further investigation, which might also include the lion in Asia, is desirable. I must confess to not having taken observations as to the direction of wind, for it has never occurred either to me or to my shikaris that this is of any importance in hunting the tiger, nor has there been any reason to think otherwise.

I have known tigers pass within twenty yards and less of picketed buffaloes without killing, although others have been killed a little farther on. The inference has been that the buffalo passed by was asleep and immobile, and thus escaped observation. Either there was no wind, or the wind must have been blowing from the buffalo towards the tiger; otherwise the buffalo would have been roused to movement by the smell of the beast of prey. Then I have walked right up to a slightly wounded tiger, which was lying down and did not detect my approach until a few feet off, when it raised its head and recognition blazed into its eyes. And I have taken off my boots and stalked to within fifteen yards of a tigress which remained ignorant of my proximity until disturbed by a bullet. Driven tigers, approaching with slow and measured tread, have come close to me without betraying any sign of having detected my presence, sometimes stopping to listen to the noise that pursued them, but scenting no danger. Those in the habit of sitting in ambush to watch for a tiger or a leopard have always taken precautions against being seen or heard, but have ignored the question of scent, and have even found no need to refrain from smoking. Some have observed that these animals are at a loss to follow a kill that has been dragged away by hand for some distance, but in such circumstances a beast will sometimes if not always track the drag slowly, scenting the trail. It would not do to deny to the tiger and the leopard some sense of smell, but that they hunt with a "winding nose" remains to be proved.

The tiger generally prefers to keep to paths or roads rather than move through cover, both for facility of seeing and to avoid the discomfort of bushes or grass brushing against its flanks. We frequently read of a tiger "springing" on its prey as though it were in the habit of launching itself through the air. It may spring from higher ground, but the prey is usually reached by a rush from a charging distance of 20 yards or so at the end of the stalk; the tiger's hind-legs do not usually leave the ground, and the quarry is seized and borne to the earth by the terrific impetus of the charge. But it may come up quietly and seize its prey. An officer walking along a jungle path with his shikari behind him heard no sound except a deep sigh, and on turning round saw a tiger with the man's neck in its jaws, standing on its hind-legs, its fore-paws on his back and chest or shoulder. In an instant it had gone with its prey.

A tiger may spring across a nullah, but it does not spring about as so often represented. It generally seizes its prey by the neck, either taking the throat in its jaws from below or seizing the back of the neck, at the same time embracing with its fore-legs the chest and shoulders of the victim, with extended claws; scratches are usually present on the fore part of the body. The great retractile claws are extended only in attack or when an animal is frightened or angered, as when fired at or wounded. Otherwise they are sheathed, and the great cat pads along on silent, cushioned feet. The claws are cleaned and smoothed from scaling by scratching on trees, which may be observed marked in this way, just as a domestic cat cleans its claws on a tree in the garden. Round the base of the claws and teeth are black lines of putrid animal matter which constitutes a virulent poison. It is often asked whether the tiger or the leopard is the more dangerous animal, and many have averred that the leopard is more to be feared, being more ready to attack when wounded, and able to conceal itself with greater facility. A leopard will certainly shrink into a very small space and take cover where a tiger would at once be visible. Both when wounded will attack with equal readiness and ferocity; but the wounds inflicted by the tiger leave little chance of recovery owing to the superior size and power of the animal's jaws and claws. Blood-poisoning is a common sequel to wounds inflicted by either animal. But the injuries by the tiger are more often immediately mortal. In one such case the man had his lower jaw carried away; his cheek-bones were crushed to pieces, and the lacerated muscles of his throat, from which his torn tongue also protruded, hung down over his chest. In fact, nothing of a face was left below the eyes.

Frequently the neck of the prey is broken in falling with the weight of the tiger. Sometimes seizure of the hind-legs, including ham-stringing, results from an attack on a fleeing animal. I shot in the Melghat Forest an emaciated blue bull whose back was deeply scored by the claws of a tiger. The prey is not killed by a stroke of the paw as sometimes represented; but a brass dish, borne on a man's back, was pierced by the claws of a tiger which charged back through the line of beaters; an angry tiger often tears down with extended claws a cloth placed on a bush to keep him within the limits of the beat.

A tiger hunting by night may make a round of many miles, visiting a number of water-holes in search of prey and to quench its thirst during these peregrinations which often follow a regular beat. By day it will lie up in dense cover where there is cool shade from the heat of the sun; it almost invariably lies up near water, and sometimes immersed up to its neck in a pool; this habit leads to the association of tigers with peafowl, so often observed, those birds being equally dependent on water, which also attracts the tiger's prey. On one occasion when I shot a tiger that emerged dripping from the bath, my followers declared that this particular animal, which we had hunted for some days, was in the habit of lying in a pool with only the tip of its tail exposed; this appendage, waving to and fro above the surface, betrayed its presence in the water; how the animal breathed was not related!

The tiger does not suck the blood of its victim. It almost invariably begins to eat at the haunches, often removing the stomach and intestine and placing them on one side as unfit for food, although this offal is devoured by hyenas, jackals, and vultures. Sometimes a whole buffalo calf of good size is eaten at a "sitting"; but when the tiger is not hungry, it may feed on the carcass for two or three days, or when already satiated may leave the kill untouched save for the death-wound in the throat; sometimes several animals in a herd are killed in quick succession.

When the tiger has killed, it usually drags its prey into cover, not only for convenience of eating but to protect it from hyenas, jackals, vultures, and other scavengers. It will break a thick rope by which an animal is tethered in order to drag the carcass away. I have known a tiger to cover the remains with leaves, and even to throw it into a pool of water, to hide it from the keen eyes of the vultures, which hunt by sight and not by scent, and may be seen circling in the sky above in search of carrion. A kill may often be detected by watching the vultures descend. If they are engaged on the carcass itself, it is certain that the beast of prey is not close by; if they are sitting on the surrounding trees, it indicates that the tiger is on the spot. I have found a dead vulture which rashly approached the kill when the tiger was at hand, and was killed by a stroke of the mighty paw. The exact position of the carcass or of the tiger may sometimes be indicated by one or more crows cawing in the tree above. The tiger may utter a roar in attacking, but is generally a silent animal, in contradistinction to the lion, and his voice is seldom heard. His deep purring may at times strike upon the ear in the forests of the night, and he has a peculiar call at times, somewhat resembling the bark of a sambar deer and therefore supposed by some to be a hunting call to attract or locate his prey ; it is, however, a call to his mate. The wounded tiger when charging gives vent to deep coughing growls or grunts ; a tiger disturbed at his kill, or turned or alarmed suddenly in a beat will utter a grunt. He will roar when charging back through a line of beaters.

CHAPTER VIII

TIGER-HUNTING

IN India at any rate the tiger is the King of Beasts. From the earliest times he has been regarded as the noblest of Indian game, and hunting him was a royal sport indulged in by the Moghul Emperors. Babar, the founder of the Moghul Empire, was one of the most interesting and remarkable characters in history, possessing, like Hadrian, the attributes of the soldier, the statesman, and the scholar. He could turn a quatrain or lop off an infidel's head with equal facility. The story of his wanderings and adventures resembles a tale from the *Arabian Nights*. He invaded India in 1526, 127 years after his ancestor Tamerlane had encamped on the dusty plains round Delhi, and nearly nineteen centuries after Alexander the Great had put to flight the elephants of Poros on the bank of the Hydaspes.

Tamerlane, or Taimur Lang, was also a mighty hunter who organised great drives for game, forming a " hunting-ring " with his armies. But he was a barbarian compared with Babar who, the historian Ferishta says, " when he had an inclination to make merry used to fill a fountain with wine, inscribing on it a verse—' Jovial days ! Blooming springs ! Old wine and young maidens ! Enjoy freely, O Babar, for life is not twice to be enjoyed ! ' " Babar, who floated down the Kabul river on a raft while his army marched through the Khyber Pass, gives in his Memoirs the following account of a tiger-hunt near Peshawar. "Early in the morning we marched. Where the road leaves the river we heard a tiger howling, and he soon came forth. The moment the horses heard the tiger's roar, they became unmanageable and galloped off with their riders, plunging down the steep slopes and precipices. The tiger retreated again into the jungle, and I ordered a buffalo to be brought and put in the wood for the purpose of luring him out. He soon issued forth again, roaring. Arrows poured down on him from every side, and I also shot my arrow. Then Kalwah Piadeh struck him with a spear, and he twisted and broke the spear with his teeth and tossed it away. The tiger had received many wounds, when Baba Yesawal, drawing his sword, came near and struck him on the head at the moment when he sprang. After this Ali Sistani pierced his loins, when he plunged into the river, where they killed him."

In the eighteenth century the Nawab Vizir of Oudh used to take the field for a hunting expedition accompanied by his court, a great part of his army, amounting to 10,000 cavalry, as many infantry, and 30 or 40 guns, as well as 800 elephants and an immense camp with camels, bullock-carts, and baggage, and a market of 60,000 people. His armoury consisted of 40 or 50 double-barrelled guns, and innumerable single guns, muskets, rifles, and pistols. Tigers were driven from their lairs by a line of elephants, the whole being manœuvred like a body of troops. On a smaller scale but in much the same style, hunting is organised to-day in Nepal and by Indian Princes for Royalty,

Viceroys, Governors, Commanders-in-Chief, and other eminent personages. In northern India, in the Terai and other foothills of the Himalayas, the forest is so dense with tall elephant-grass and bush that shooting has to be done from elephant-back.

The methods adopted by the inhabitants for ridding a district of predatory tigers preying on their cattle or themselves are not without interest. In Mysore and in other parts of the country, the cover in which the tiger lies is surrounded by nets, the animal being then disturbed from its siesta and speared when it comes up against the nets. In the time of the Emperor Akbar, and in Sambalpur as recently as forty years ago, masses of leaves smeared with bird-lime were laid on the paths or other localities frequented by the tiger. The animal, tormented by the leaves adhering to his paws, would try to rub them off, bite at them, and get them sticking all over his eyes, head, and body, when the hunters came up and speared him. Tigers were also caught in cages like a great mouse-trap with a compartment in the middle for a live goat or other bait; or in pits, or killed by a dropping pike or by poisoned arrows discharged from a platform in a tree. The poison was said to be obtained from a tree known as tiger-poison, which has not been identified. The shikaris of Dinajpur used to travel all over Bengal, killing tigers for the sake of the government reward, which they would sometimes obtain twice over by taking the head of a tiger to one district officer and the skin to another.

To spear a tiger is a formidable undertaking, and it has often been said that the only man who has performed this feat was Sir James Outram, "the Bayard of India," who was as good a sportsman as he was a soldier. But another famous soldier, Colonel R. R. Gillespie, in 1810, attempted to spear a tiger that had been caged in Mysore. The door of the cage was turned towards open country, and when it was raised the tiger crept out and, looking round, immediately turned on the guard of six sepoys who had brought the cage. The nearest man presented his bayonet which entered the tiger's side and threw it over, but in an instant the animal recovered itself and, twisting the bayonet off the weapon, knocked down all the sepoys one after another like a set of ninepins, putting its paws on one man's shoulders and biting out four of his teeth.

Colonel Gillespie then rode at the beast and delivered his spear without much effect. Twenty peons now advanced, and one ran up behind the tiger and with his long straight sword cut it over the tail. The animal turned and received a stab in the mouth, and this brave man, when the tiger rushed at him, retreated so as to draw it into the midst of his comrades, who despatched it with a hundred wounds. After this tigers were often supplied for spearing, and the Raja of Mysore sent one to be hunted on the race-course by a party of officials. Mr. Cole, the Resident, speared him four times, scarcely drawing blood. Others speared the beast, which was at last driven into a small tank and drowned. Next day two tigers were procured, one of which was killed by Mr. Cole ; the other chased Major Russell of the Madras Cavalry, who was nearly overtaken when two natives ran in between and one was killed by the beast with a single blow. The tiger then retreated under the race-course stand, into which a woman and child had crept for safety, but they escaped leaving a cloth which was snatched by the tiger; it was then shot with a pistol by Colonel Welsh and done to death with spears. Altogether the episode was unpleasant.

The finest sport in Central and Southern India is to beat out the tiger in the heat of the day. Sixty or seventy years ago this used to be done on elephant-back, the hunter having his own elephant and the tiger being walked up in the vicinity of its kill or followed up and shot. But the more general way of shooting in the Deccan is for the tiger to be driven out by a line of beaters towards the gun, posted on a rock, a tree, or other point of vantage. It is better to take up a commanding position instead of standing on the ground, not so much for security as for increasing the chance of a shot. The tiger does not look up, but is quick to perceive the slightest movement within his range of vision, such as the raising of the rifle to the shoulder. Few tigers are shot on foot.

Another method is to take a position of concealment in a tree over a live animal, such as a young buffalo or a goat, or the remains of the tiger's prey. It usually returns to renew its feast on the carcass before sunset, when a shot may be obtained, or an electric light may be switched on if the beast returns after dark. In all these methods, in the absence of a natural kill, it is necessary to tie up as bait an animal, generally a young buffalo, after killing which the tiger will lie up in the adjacent jungle, if the spot has been well chosen. In this method of hunting tigers there is little or no luck, a factor that enters into all the affairs of life much less than is commonly supposed. Someone may say, "How lucky you are to have shot so many tigers!" They do not understand the knowledge of the animal's habits, gained by careful observation and thought, the enterprise, the careful preparation, the infinite labour, and other matters which have contributed to success. This is especially the case with the lone hunter, inspired by the natural instinct for adventure, who with a small camp and a few native followers ranges the jungles during the hottest season of the year, and as the fruit of his own exertions may get a bag of 12 or 14 tigers during a six weeks' expedition.

The organization of such an expedition entails a careful selection of shikaris and other followers, the collection of information, involving a knowledge of the character and prejudices of the people of the country as well as of their language, and of the nature of the wild beasts. Then in old days one had to ride 60 or 70 miles to the first camp, sent on a week ahead to save time, and the distance covered in a day's ride for the same purpose. Nowadays perhaps the effort would be less severe in all respects owing to the introduction of motor-transport. The journey was made in the hot weather, with the thermometer registering anything up to 110 degrees in the shade. It was a strenuous undertaking. But the joy of it! To pitch the tent, only eight feet square, beneath shady trees on the bank of the river, shrunk to a silver thread with occasional pools at this dry season of the year in the month of March or April. To hear once more the sweetest of music—the voices of the forest—the bark of the deer, the shrill cry of the peafowl, the jungle cocks crowing defiance to one another, and the stridulation of cicadas filling the forest with incessant screech. To see a herd of dappled deer come down to drink within view of the camp; and at night perhaps to listen to the deep purr of a prowling tiger, or the harsh grating cry of a leopard in search of prey. Such scenes and sounds will never be forgotten until the hunter departs for the Happy Hunting Grounds.

Then to look for tracks, to inspect waterholes in the valleys among the hills where game is plentiful and where there are cool retreats; to picket out the unfortunate buffalo calves that have to serve as bait in likely spots indicated by tracks, and where there are shade and water to keep the tiger to his lair after he has found the meal provided for him. The "bait" suffers little, and when wounded and knocked over has been known to resume grazing at once. The line for the prospective beat in each locality must be inspected, for success depends on attention to all details. All this may entail a tramp of many miles, perhaps fifteen or more under a scorching sun, but there is no royal road to success and the labour is well repaid, not only in bringing the game to bag, but in fresh lessons of the habits of wild beasts constantly to be learnt from the book of nature.

In the arrangements after the tiger has been located, the chief secret is to drive the beast in the direction it would naturally take, not towards open ground that it will not face. The novice may find difficulty in this, but the experienced man who possesses an eye for country and takes all circumstances into consideration should be able to avoid mistakes. If an attempt is made to drive a tiger against its will towards country unsuited to its habits, it may break back through the line of stops or beaters; at best the chance of a shot is spoilt; at worst, one or more men may be killed or injured. Then stops have to be posted to turn the game in any attempt to break out of the beat, and a good post has to be selected for the gun. Stops should be trustworthy men, and care is essential in choosing and posting them. All this entails much hard work, but the labour is a pleasure in view of the results; that which is easily gained has less value. There is in all this little or no luck; in my experience there is none.

The shot should not be taken until the tiger is passing, otherwise it may be turned back upon the beaters. The tendency is for the animal when wounded to go on straight in its original direction. An unwounded tiger rarely charges. In the course of many months spent in pursuit of these beasts, driven out and sometimes shot on foot, only one instance of an unwounded tiger seizing a man has come within my experience; that was the exceptional case of an animal which had lost itself in unwonted surroundings and entered a compound at Jalna as previously related. Under provocation, when harried in a beat, tigers have occasionally charged back roaring through the line, but no man has been struck down.

Many fatalities have occurred in tiger-hunting, but they have almost without exception been the work of beasts that had been wounded and were followed up on foot. An example of the manner of such accidents may be taken from my own experience. A tiger was driven straight towards my post in a tree some twelve feet from the ground, and the shot, fired too soon, struck him at an acute angle between the shoulders, making a long superficial cut in his back. The beast dashed on, a second bullet missed, and he disappeared in tall grass and tree jungle. Then a leopard walked out of the same beat, and was shot dead with one bullet. The wounded tiger had entered a small nullah where tracks and spots of blood marked his course, but after a hundred yards of this tracking, with tall grass affording concealment on either side of the winding course, the trail became too dangerous to follow. A few hundred yards farther on the nullah made a sharp bend into bare, burnt ground for a score of paces. I made for the bend and came suddenly on the tiger lying under a tree six feet off. He raised his head, his eyes blazed as they met mine, and in an instant he was dead with a bullet through the heart. This was a typical instance of escape from what might well have been a fatal accident; but my approach had been silent.

The death in 1930 of Colonel Hastings from wounds inflicted by a tiger recalls many such fatalities, which bear a general resemblance to one another. The animal is wounded and followed up. Usually it has taken cover in more or less dense jungle, where a charging beast is neither easily seen nor easily stopped, as those are well aware who have faced a charge made with determination and generally at close quarters. In this instance a sleeping tiger was fired at and wounded. After a considerable interval, which is advisable to afford time for a wound to stiffen, or even to have fatal results, the officer followed up the tiger, accompanied by a shikari carrying a spare rifle, a bearer or native body-servant, and half a dozen beaters, no doubt local peasants. The ground was rocky, affording plenty of concealment to a lurking animal, and there was scattered bush. The party advanced, throwing stones, a sure way of inducing a charge, and the tiger came on from a distance of twenty yards; the sportsman missed with his first barrel, inflicted a slight wound with his second, and was then pulled down and badly mauled. The man with the spare rifle bolted, as naturally did the unarmed beaters; it is unfortunate that the bearer was not carrying the spare rifle, for this brave man, with the devotion so often displayed by his class, beat off the tiger with a stick, dragged his master away, fetched the rifle from the shikari, and finished off the animal. This last action was especially satisfactory, for according to Indian ideas the victim is sure to die if the tiger survives. It was fourteen hours before any surgical aid could be rendered, long enough for blood-poisoning to set in, as there were no antiseptics and the patient had to be carried six miles to the road, and wait for a lorry to take him to hospital.

Such accidents must sometimes occur, but no doubt can often be avoided or their results may be minimised by due precautions. Each one presents special features, although conforming in general character. While the victim may be a novice, experienced hunters are apt to become careless and have not infrequently met with disaster. Indeed, it has been said that one has only to continue the practice of following wounded and dangerous animals long enough to meet with disaster in the end. But accidents have generally been owing to neglect of elementary precautions, or to rashness due to long immunity. The hunter should first see that his rifle is efficient, and should do his best to disable his game with the first shot; a second or more shots should be put in if the beast is still active. But instances occur when a wounded beast must be followed, and the precaution of first seeing that the weapon is ready should never be neglected. This may seem superfluous advice, but in 1894 a sportsman was killed by a tiger which charged from a distance of eighty yards, and it was found that he had not reloaded his rifle after firing two shots in the first instance, although an hour had elapsed before he followed up the game. Two companions were with him, and one killed the beast just as it seized him by the shoulder, its jaws closing so tightly that they had to be wrenched asunder to release him. It is best on such occasions to have the habit of taking out the cartridges, examining the rifle, and reloading immediately before starting to follow the tracks.

Several methods have been recommended in dealing with wounded tigers and leopards. Blood tracks are less likely with modern small-bore rifles than with the old heavy weapons having less velocity and greater striking surface. In many cases blood does not take one far, but a wounded animal of this hot-blooded species, impatient of heat and thirst, does not often go far. The chief object is to obtain a shot before the wounded beast charges; for in most localities a charge is usually from close quarters and not easy to stop. A rifle taking a heavy bullet is more likely to deliver a knock-out blow. A 12-bore gun loaded with buckshot is good for checking the charge of a leopard; whether it will stop a tiger is doubtful, as anyone will understand who has seen the power and fury of a tiger's charge.

Sometimes a wounded tiger may be located with the aid of a herd of buffaloes, driven into the cover; but they will not always scent the tiger, and have been known to pass near it without detecting its presence, as I found in the case of a leopard. An instance of the danger of this method occurred on an island in the Pench river some years ago, where one morning a police officer shot three out of four tigers without trouble. A herd of buffaloes was put in to dislodge the fourth, a big tiger which had been slightly wounded; the tiger repeatedly charged from end to end of the island, and rushed over the backs of the buffaloes to get at the herdsman and another man with him, both of whom were killed before the beast was shot.

The pursuit of a wounded tiger should never be abandoned. Such an animal becomes a danger to the countryside and will kill anyone who passes near it. In one instance a sportsman was examining the body of a boy who had been killed in this manner when the tiger attacked and mortally injured him. Personally I have always preferred to follow directly on the tracks with one or two trusty armed men. Look-out men may be sent up trees at intervals to observe the ground in front, but they are apt to see the tiger in every bush. Certainly the coloration very often blends remarkably with the surrounding jungle, especially of panthers in the chequered light and shade of bushes. A shikari should attend to the tracking, or attention may be distracted at the moment when the beast should be seen and shot. Much depends on the nature of the ground, but generally the throwing of stones into cover is to incite a charge and invite disaster when a careful approach may enable a shot to be put in before the animal moves. In a bush-filled nullah with steep banks one should move along the top, and stones may be thrown in to provoke an up-hill charge, which is not difficult to stop. To follow up a wounded tiger or leopard must always be a dangerous undertaking, but with care it is usually possible to bring the hunt to a successful issue without accident. Every sportsman should have in his possession carbolic acid, iodine, bandages, and other surgical appliances for the treatment of wounds.

From old books on big-game hunting, it might be gathered that there is perpetual war between man and nature. But man and wild animals are not always at strife, and tigers are not entirely pernicious animals. In early days, when the natives had most primitive weapons, and there were few English sportsmen in remote districts, they no doubt suffered much from the depredations of wild beasts, but then carnivorous animals found more ample supplies of natural food. Tigers have their uses. The weaklings of the species on which they prey are probably their first victims, and it is well that these should not survive to reduce the quality of the race by breeding weak descendants. They are useful in keeping within bounds the numbers of animals such as pig and nilgai which devastate the husbandman's crops. But the balance of nature should be maintained, and if herbivorous animals are exterminated, as they are likely to be where the use of arms is freely permitted, the tigers turn for sustenance to domesticated beasts, and even to man himself. Nor does the hunting of wild beasts involve continual hand-to-claw encounters, as might be gathered from some works of fiction such as were in vogue fifty or sixty years ago, from which it might be inferred that not only lions, tigers, and leopards were always ready to attack man at sight, but that such comparatively timid animals as bison, buffalo, and rhinoceros were always charging about in pursuit of the hunter.

Nearly every year brings its toll of fatalities to sportsmen tiger-hunting. There was a number of such deaths in 1887. Mr. Hughes, a Bombay civilian, was bitten in over thirty places by a tiger, and died next day. Major Lyons fired at a tiger in a cave ; it charged out, seized him by the leg, and carried him 200 yards, when he thrust his rifle into its throat and it made off with the weapon. A few years afterwards Sir James Dormer, Commander-in-Chief of the Madras Army, was following up a wounded tiger near Ootacamund, when it seized him by the foot, inflicting slight wounds, but he died from blood-poisoning. Captain Whistler was fatally wounded by a tiger near Asirgarh. His sepoy orderly behaved most gallantly, running the tiger through with a spear while it was on his officer's body. In 1894 Lieutenant Sexton, when out with Captain R. W. Burton and another officer in the Godavery jungles, was charged by a wounded tigress which seized his arm and shoulder, and on the instant the beast was shot dead by Burton, but Sexton died next day. Such instances might be multiplied a hundredfold.

In 1926 two East Indian Railway officials, Messrs. Lewis and Bathgate, went after a tiger which they met suddenly in a clearing in the forest. Lewis fired and wounded the tiger, which made off but turned on them as they followed it. Lewis was knocked down, and Bathgate, having no rifle, attacked the tiger with a hatchet ; it seized him and tore off his arm, and then turned on and killed his companion. Some years ago Mr. Bell, a Deputy Commissioner in the Central Provinces, was following a tiger he had wounded, accompanied by his wife. The tiger charged and seized him, Mrs. Bell bravely rushed forward and fired at the tiger, and then clubbed her rifle and beat it off. Her husband died the same evening.

Two military officers, Messrs. Rice and Elliot, followed a wounded tigress which left blood and foot-prints for some distance, but all tracks were lost in an open space in the jungle. Their men had followed in a body, but when the tracks ceased the two advanced a short distance ahead to examine the ground. A sudden roar startled them, and the tigress charged out at full speed while Elliot was stooping down looking for tracks. Rice fired two shots, and the beast swerved and seized Elliot who was twenty yards off on his left. The shikari then handed Rice his spare gun, but two more shots had little effect, for the tigress began dragging Elliot off by the upper part of his arm towards the ditch in which she had been lying, growling all the time. It was some time before another shot could be fired for fear of hitting the prostrate man, but at length the animal dropped dead with a bullet in the head. Elliot was pulled out from under the tigress; he was terribly mauled, but had to some extent covered himself with his rifle, which was much damaged and clawed. He escaped with his life. It is a good plan for a body of men to follow, although I have myself preferred to leave the beaters behind. But an animal seldom charges a crowd. In this instance Elliot made a common mistake in looking for tracks when he should have been ready for a charge.

Two remarkable accidents in which ladies were concerned took place some years ago. In tiger-shooting there is no "safety first," for the first thing is to kill the animal, and there is no place for women. Mr.

Sneyde, an irrigation officer, was on tour in the Central Provinces, accompanied by his brother and sister. A beat was organized for a tiger, Mr. Sneyde and his sister sitting in one tree and the brother in another. The tiger came out between the two trees and was wounded but got away. After warning their sister not to leave her tree, the two brothers went after the animal, and again wounded it. Again following, they came to an open space and found the dead bodies of the tiger and their sister. Hearing the second shot she had got down from her perch, no doubt assuming that the tiger had been killed, and met it face to face with fatal result.

In January 1926, Mr. Smythies, a Forest Officer, was out shooting in the Terai with his wife who was in a tree while her husband was on foot with the beaters. She fired at and wounded a tiger that broke cover near her, and tried to break back, but was again driven towards her. This time it sprang up the tree, and began climbing to the platform of branches on which she was seated. She pushed the rifle down its throat, but it missfired; fortunately Mr. Smythies came on the scene in time to finish off the beast, which had actually climbed on to the platform.

Usually there is safety in a tree at a height of about fourteen feet from the ground, but this depends on the nature of the tree, and although such a heavy-bodied animal is not a good climber, many instances of tigers climbing trees are on record. In one case a tiger, struck on the back of the head by a bullet the previous evening, was found dead on the lower branch of a pipal tree (*Ficus religiosa*) 15 feet from the ground. The marks of the claws showed that it had scrambled up cat-fashion, and had run to the end of the branch, where it lay down and died with its legs on either side. In another instance a hunted tigress climbed up and seized a man in a tree 20 feet from the ground, and then lost her balance and fell.

A sportsman heard of a tiger sitting in a tree, blockaded by villagers. He rode to the place, 500 yards from the village, and saw men picketed round a large pipal, a spearman standing almost beneath it. When he approached within 100 yards, "there appeared, standing on a sturdy branch high aloft in the tree, the tiger, erect and calm and fearless, with black, yellow, and white stripes looking beautiful in high relief." It was 25 feet above the ground, and when shot caught a lower branch with both arms in falling, hung for a minute, and then dropped dead. Another tiger attacked a buffalo near a village at daybreak, and was driven off by the herd-boy. The villagers turned out, the tiger got up a tree where it was picketed by the people, who sent word to a planter. He approached on an elephant, and shot the tiger as it stood on a branch at a higher level than the howdah, about nineteen feet. In an instance near Ootacamund, a tigress mounted to the top branches of a tall tree 30 feet from the ground, off which she was knocked with two shots. But she again got up the tree and stood looking down and exposing her chest to another shot, which finished her.

A remarkable story appeared in the Calcutta *Statesman* some 15 years ago. Mr. and Mrs. F. were on their way to Calcutta from Assam, having to drive 35 miles to the station in a dog-cart. The train was due to leave the station at one o'clock in the morning. On their road a tiger had taken up a beat and was so troublesome that all traffic had to be stopped at sunset, as the tiger had taken a number of bullocks out of passing carts. The tiger's patrol was on a three-mile stretch between Kotiatuli Post Office and the station of Chaparmukh on the near side of a river that was bridged. Once across the bridge, travellers were supposed to be safe. At about half-past ten the party left a bungalow where they had dined, nine miles from the station. Mr. and Mrs. F. sat in front, Mr. F. driving, the lady with the child in her arms, and an ayah and syce sitting behind. They were in an American four-wheeler. The horse and harness were lit up by two brilliant lamps, which shone on the road ahead and lighted up the drain and banks on each side. They reached the river and crossed the bridge, when Mr. F. said to his wife: "That's all right, you needn't be frightened any more." Just as he spoke, his wife said: "What's that?" In the light cast by the lamp they saw a huge tiger galloping alongside the trap, its back on a level with the tops of the wheels. As they sat looking, mute with awe, the tiger moved on to the pony's head and they next saw its great paws round the pony's neck, the head jerked upwards, and in a moment it fell dead without a movement. The tiger had attacked on the driving side, and it deliberately got hold of the pony just in front of the withers, and began to drag it and the trap with its five occupants across the road, at the edge of which it entered the jungle without much effort. Probably it could not see the occupants of the trap, as the light to some extent blinded it. The trap had not been dragged far off the road when the axle caught the stump of a tree and the procession came to a stop.

Mr. F. then regained his presence of mind. He got

out of the trap and said: "Give me the child." Even at that critical moment, the mother said: "Be careful, she's asleep," and stepped down after her husband. The whole incident occurred so quickly that there was no outcry, and even the talk had been in whispers. The whole party got clear of the trap and started running up the road. They went to an empty house close by. It was autumn and the night was cold, but a fire was lighted and, sleeping and sitting dozing, the long hours slowly passed. At the first streak of dawn the weary father and mother were awakened by the rattle of bullock-carts on the road; when these approached Mr. F. stopped them and told the drivers what had happened. With one or two men he went to the scene of the night's adventure, and there found that the head of the pony had been eaten away. Messengers were sent back to the house where they had dined the night before. When the harness was removed from the dead pony, the headstall was lying intact on the ground, though how the beast managed to drag the head away was a mystery. The body of the pony was poisoned, and with some other people the travellers went to get elephants; on their return they found that the tiger had made a meal off it, but they beat the surrounding jungle without result. Some weeks later the carcass of a large tiger was found at the edge of a pool where it had slaked its thirst, and had died from the effects of the poison. It was fortunate that this tiger was not a man-eater, for tigers sometimes waylay carts on the forest roads and take the bullocks out of them, like one on the main road in the Melghat Forest; in hopes of getting a shot at it I travelled more than once in a cart, but never saw the beast.

If some of our daily papers had been in existence in October 1857 they would have had some fine headlines, such a " Man-eater in Ratcliff Highway," where an incident rivalling in sensation that of the murders described by De Quincey took place. A tiger just landed in London Docks escaped from the cage in which it was confined in Jamrach's yard. The tiger walked out into the street, and a little boy who was playing there went up and patted the beast, and was promptly seized by the shoulder and carried off. The famous animal dealer just then arrived on the scene and grasped the tiger by the loose skin of its neck, but it started off galloping up the street, carrying the boy as a cat carries a mouse, Jamrach holding on and running alongside. Jamrach then tripped the tiger up by the hind-leg, threw himself upon it, and held on to its ears, the three lying in a heap, the boy still firmly gripped in the beast's jaws. Jamrach called out to one of his men to bring a crow-bar, with which he beat the tiger over the nose, making it drop the boy ; it ran back to its cage. The child, who was not much hurt, recovered in eight days. Later this same tiger walked out of its cage in a menagerie, and entering a neighbouring compartment inhabited by a lion, took the King of Beasts by the throat and killed him in a few minutes.

CHAPTER IX

THE MAN-EATERS OF SAGAR ISLAND

THE dense and impenetrable jungle of the Sundarbans, comprising marsh, morass, and forest, has always been famous as the haunt of man-eating tigers. It harbours other wild beasts. Buffalo and deer, pig and antelope, have found there a safe retreat. It is intersected by a network of streams; it contains no villages, and is little frequented by man. It has seldom been visited even by enterprising English sportsmen, for the game it contains is practically inaccessible in this intricate jungle. Tigers sometimes swim across the channels of the Ganges delta, and have even been know to board boats upon the water.

On the eastward side of the Hughli channel, through which the ships of all nations have sailed or steamed on the way to Calcutta, lies Sagar Island, a large tract of jungle-covered ground. In the days of sailing-ships it was sometimes visited by people from Calcutta, or by landing-parties from the boats of passing vessels, when they anchored off the shore. But it is probable that it was generally given a wide berth after the death from the jaws of man-eating tigers of two European visitors towards the latter end of the eighteenth century.

The first of these tragedies is recorded in the *Annual Register* for 1787 in a letter dated from Calcutta on

October 12th, 1786, and it is worthy of remark that the record states that "this melancholy accident shows that a tyger is not always deterred from approaching fire." A small vessel bound from Ganjam to Calcutta, being longer on the passage than was expected, ran out of provisions and water: being near Sagar Island, the Europeans, six in number, went on shore in search of refreshments. There were some coconuts on the island, in quest of which they strayed a considerable way. Darkness coming on and the vessel being at a distance, it was thought safer to take up a night's lodging in the ruins of an old pagoda than to return to the vessel. A large fire was lighted and it was agreed that two of the number should keep watch by turns, to alarm the rest in case of danger which they had reason to apprehend from the wild appearance of the place. It fell to the lot of one Dawson, late a silversmith and engraver of Calcutta, to be on watch. In the night a tiger rushed over the fire and, seizing Dawson, sprang off with him in its jaws, but struck its head against the side of the pagoda, rebounding with its prey upon the fire over which they rolled over one another once or twice before the man was carried off. In the morning they found the thighs and legs of the unfortunate victim at some distance, mangled and stripped of flesh.

It was unfortunate that the fate of this man was not known to another party who, in the ship *Ardasier Shaw*, anchored off Sagar Island on December 22nd, 1792. Or if they were aware of the tragedy of six years before, they did not grasp the significance of its lesson which proved the uselessness of fire as a protection against a determined man-eating wild beast. Their story was related in a letter from Captain Consar, one of the party, published in the *Annual Register* for 1793. The others were Captain George Downey, Lieutenant Pyefinch, and Mr. Munro of the East India Company's Service, a son of Sir Hector Munro. They all landed on Sagar Island to shoot deer. Captain Consar wrote: " We saw innumerable tracks of tigers and deer; but still we were induced to pursue our sport and did so the whole day. About half-past three we sat down on the edge of the jungle to eat some cold meat, sent to us from the ship, and had just commenced our meal when Mr. Pyefinch and a black servant told us there was a fine deer within six yards of us. Captain Downey and I immediately jumped up to take our guns; mine was nearest, and I had just laid hold of it when I heard a roar like thunder, and saw an immense royal tiger spring on the unfortunate Munro, who was sitting down; in a moment his head was in the beast's mouth, and it rushed into the jungle with him with as much ease as I could lift a kitten, tearing him through the thickest bushes and trees, everything yielding to its monstrous force. The agonies of horror, regret, and fear rushed on me at once, for there were two tigers; the only effort I could make was to fire at the tiger, though the poor youth was still in its mouth. I relied partly on Providence, partly on my own aim, and fired a musket, saw the tiger stagger and agitated, and cried out so immediately. Captain Downey then fired two shots and I one more; we retired from the jungle and a few minutes afterwards Mr. Munro came up to us all over blood, and fell. We took him on our backs to the boat, and got every medical attendance for him from the *Valentine*, Indiaman, which lay at anchor near the island, but in vain. He lived twenty-four hours after, but in the extreme of torture; his head and skull were all torn and broken to pieces, and he was also wounded by the animal's claws all over the neck and shoulders; but it was better to take him away, though irrecoverable, than to leave him to be devoured limb by limb. We have just read the funeral service over his body and committed it to the deep. He was an amiable and promising youth.

I must observe there was a large fire blazing close to us composed of ten or a dozen whole trees; I made it myself on purpose to keep the tigers off, as I had always heard it would. There were eight or ten of the natives with us, and many shots had been fired at the place, and much noise and laughing at the time, but this ferocious animal disregarded all.

The human mind cannot form an idea of the scene; it turned my very soul within me. The beast was about four and a half feet high and nine feet long. His head appeared as large as that of an ox, his eyes darting fire, and his roar when he first seized his prey will never be out of my recollection. We had scarcely pushed our boat from that cursed shore when the tigress made her appearance, almost raging mad, and remained on the sand as long as the distance would allow me to see her."

These two stories are typical instances of the futility of trusting to fire for safety from the attacks of wild beasts. They confirm many other similar instances given in this book, and they are of special interest as furnishing examples of fires both by day and by night. Yet it is remarkable that, in spite of all such examples, which amount to proof, the erroneous idea still prevails that travellers are protected from attack by the mere presence of fire. This misconception probably had its origin in the old-established error that the great cats will attack any human being they happen to meet with, or will search out man as an object of attack. In innumerable books of travel and sport are references to the assumed protection of a camp-fire, while in other parts of the same volumes may be found proof that this confers no immunity. It is an assumption almost universally accepted.

In South America the traveller has little to fear from the jaguar and the puma, which perhaps accounts for so observant a naturalist as W. H. Hudson accepting the popular idea without comment. In his *Naturalist in La Plata* he remarks on the fascinating and confusing effect that light has on animals. This is known to every poacher who hunts birds and beasts with a lantern, or salmon with a torch, both in the British Isles and in the South of India. Hudson tells us that the flashing light of the fire-fly warns raptorial insects and is for the moment a protection, " as the camp-fire the traveller lights in a district abounding with beasts of prey." Then he says that the camp-fires actually serve to attract beasts of prey, but " the confusion and fear caused by the bright glare makes it safe for the traveller to lie down and sleep in the light." It is difficult to find any evidence of confusion and fear on the part of man-eaters in the many recorded instances of men taken from beside camp-fires, and with these experiences before us it is certainly not safe to lie down and sleep with no other protection when there is a man-eater about. No doubt the fire attracts, and consequently may itself be a danger, but the traveller had better not trust to the glare for safety ; should he do so he may have a rude awakening—if he ever awakes again! But whether there is a fire or not, the camp is safe unless there is a man-eater in the neighbourhood. This is the experience of those who have slept in the open for the sake of the coolness in tropical hot nights where lions, tigers, or leopards abound.

In India the present writer has heard tigers moaning near by, as Mr. Roosevelt described the lions moaning near his camp in Africa—but it never occurred to him that it was unsafe to sleep outside the tent or to have any camp-fire kept up at night, although the harsh cry of the leopard was nightly heard not far off; these animals would approach quite close to the camp; one even came to drink at a trough near his bed in the middle of the night, and paid a visit again on the next night. Undoubtedly it is wise to have fires, and watchers beside them, when the camp is in the haunts of a man-eater. But travellers would be well-advised to trust to neither fire nor light as a protection. The light is useful to reveal to the watcher the approach of the man-eater, which will keep at a distance when it knows that it is observed, or it can be shot or driven off. Only it is not the camp-fire itself, but the sentry or watcher beside it, that furnishes an element of protection against the beast of prey.

In the case of the Sagar Island man-eaters, the parties would have been safer had they bivouacked in open ground away from the jungle, for the dense cover enabled the tiger to approach unobserved. This kind of protection was recognised in former days when roads in India were more haunted by man-eating tigers than they are now. In the time of Warren Hastings a new road was cut through the districts of Ramgarh, Raghunathpur, and Bandbissanpur to shorten by nearly

200 miles the route from Calcutta to Benares. The old route followed the course of the Ganges. The engineer who carried out the work was Captain Charles Rankin, and he and after him his brother were allowed an annual sum by the Government for keeping up the road, and a further payment for destroying the jungle for a distance of fifty yards on either side of it. For it passed through a wild forest region infested by tigers, and fifty clear yards precluded a tiger from approaching in daylight unobserved within charging distance of the wayfarer.

A curious incident in Captain Consar's story of the death of Munro, was the pursuit of the party by the tigress, and its behaviour on the beach. In this the man-eater, whether tiger or tigress, and the narrator said that there were two tigers, behaved as these animals generally do, and, baulked of its prey, followed in the hope of retrieving the corpse. The same habit is observed in the case of other man-eaters, both lions and tigers. It is interesting to recall that on August 19th, 1798, the ship *Fitzwilliam*, carrying the future Duke of Wellington and the headquarters of his regiment, struck on Sagar reef, and was got off, as Colonel Arthur Wellesley wrote, by the bodily strength of the men of the 33rd. If the weather had not been moderate all must have been lost. Those who escaped drowning might have fallen victims to man-eating tigers which infested the jungles of Sagar Island.

Surgeon Daniel Johnson, in his book on *Indian Field Sports*, writing in about 1800 of the road made in the time of Warren Hastings, relates that soon after leaving Calcutta the route traversed the Chittra Ghat, a pass through the mountains. The new road often passed over ravines which afforded shelter to beasts of prey. At every village near the passes were stationed *ghatwars* to accompany travellers through the *ghats* or passes. They had a strange appearance, being generally covered with the skin of a tiger or leopard, and carried a bow and arrows ornamented with peacocks' feathers, a large shield, a spear or matchlock, and a sword. These people gave more confidence than protection. They were given land and an allowance by the Raja and were also tipped by travellers.

Tigers were in those days very numerous and destructive, whole villages being depopulated in the Ramgarh district. Surgeon Johnson relates that he sat up at night over a bullock to watch for a tiger, a *kulassi*, or tent-pitcher, being with him. At midnight an owl perched over their heads and hooted; then a jackal came along and uttered the peculiar call which these animals make when attendant on a beast of prey. The superstitious native, alarmed by these omens, begged him not to shoot if the tiger did come, or one of them would certainly be killed. They heard the tiger pass close by, but not in sight. A week later the bullocks started on the march taking the tents with the *kulassi*. Suddenly the bullock-drivers heard a horrible roar, followed by screams, and saw a tiger run over a small hill with the *kulassi* in its mouth. The bullocks threw off their loads and ran off in different directions; the men were panic-stricken, and it was some minutes before they could articulate. They then said that as the *kulassi* was driving the hindmost bullock through a nullah, the tiger sprang on him from behind a bush, and knocked him down; but owing to the nature of the ground, it passed over him after delivering the blow. Then the tiger returned, took the man up in his mouth by the thigh and made off with him at full speed with his head dangling on the ground. They followed for more than a mile, and found the corpse with all the entrails torn out and the flesh of one thigh and leg devoured. All believed that the owl was the omen of his death, of which the jackal gave vocal warning.

A tigress with two cubs lurked about the Katkamsandy Pass and killed a man, sometimes two, almost every day. Ten or twelve of these were post-runners, and communication between Calcutta and the Upper Provinces was almost cut off. A gentleman was travelling up the new road at this time in a palanquin carried by eight bearers, with two linkmen and two others carrying provisions and baggage. Early in the morning the tigress was seen, but the traveller urged his men to go on ; so they put down the palanquin and ran away, and he had to return to Hazaribagh. On another occasion a jemadar (native officer) and 40 soldiers were escorting treasure from Hazaribagh to Chittra, when in the middle of the pass they saw the tigress lying in the road. Having no orders to fire, the jemadar marched back to cantonments for instructions, and the commandant ordered him to fix bayonets and return, but the tigress had then gone.

On the same road two Brinjaras, the gypsies of India, were driving a string of laden bullocks, when the rear man was seized by a tiger. This was observed by a herdsman, who ran and cut at the tiger with his sword ; the beast dropped the Brinjara and seized the herdsman, whose buffaloes then turned on the tiger and drove it off, but too late to save his life. The first man recovered. Then an elderly man and his wife were each carrying home a bundle of wood. As they were resting their burdens on the ground, the man heard a noise, and on looking round saw a tiger running off with the woman in its mouth. He ran after it and struck it on the back with an axe, which made the tiger drop her. She was taken in to the district hospital; one breast was torn off, the other lacerated, and there were several deep wounds in the back of her neck, but she recovered in six months.

Another victim was an old Mahomedan priest, who was travelling at midday on horseback, within a few miles of Chittra, with his son, an athletic young man, walking beside him, when they heard a tiger roaring. The son urged his father to hasten, but the priest said that there was no danger, and the tiger would not molest them. He began to offer prayers, in the course of which the tiger charged, knocked him off his horse, and carried him away. The son ran after the tiger and cut at it with his sword; it dropped the old man, picked up the son, and made off into the jungle. The old priest was carried into Chittra, where he died the same day; the son was never heard of again.

It is fortunate that in course of time English sportsmen killed a great many of these animals. One Mr. Henry Ramus, Judge on Circuit in Behar, was said to have shot 360 tigers at the beginning of the last century, and as the numbers were reduced there must have been a reduction also in the bills of mortality, but at that early period statistics of deaths from wild animals were not compiled. There were many stone cairns to be seen along the roads in Bengal, marking the places where people had been killed. When a man was carried off by a tiger, a stick was erected with a piece of coloured cloth at the top as a warning to travellers. Every passer-by threw a stone on the spot, and large heaps were accumulated. Early in the last century such heaps were abundant in the Ramgarh district.

When tigers infested a particular road or pass a Hindu *yogi* would erect a temporary hut near and remain in it all day. Travellers used to assemble; the *yogi* would sacrifice a fowl, over which he would say a prayer, offering it to the deity on behalf of the company so that they might not become food for tigers. Each traveller gave him something. They then journeyed on with perfect confidence; if one was killed by a tiger, the Hindu said that his sins were too great to admit of the deity receiving his intercession.

Tigers must have been terribly destructive to both people and cattle before the advent of English sportsmen, among whom the district officers were conspicuous and did much to keep down the numbers of these animals. Thus Buchanan Hamilton wrote of the Gorakhpur district, that when the English took possession of the country, tigers were bold and numerous; soon after that event a sentinel was carried off even in the middle of the town of Gorakhpur. But tigers soon became less bold and, several Europeans of the station being keen sportsmen, their numbers had been greatly reduced. There is a terrible account of the year 1769, which was a famine year, when, most of the herbivorous animals having perished, the tigers were famishing, and great numbers infested the town of Bhiwapur, where in a very short time they killed 400 of the inhabitants; the survivors fled, and for some years the town was deserted. A fine sportsman, Mr. Parry Okeden, and his friends, when stationed in Moradabad, killed over 300 tigers between the years 1823 and 1841, as recorded in his diary.

In 1876 a family of tigers destroyed a large number of people in the country to the south of Hazaribagh, escaping all the sportsmen who hunted them. A great expedition accompanied by some English soldiers went after them, and a wide extent of country was beaten without success. It was related that an officer travelling in a palanquin through their beat at night employed a double relay of torch-bearers, and also had some men to keep up a tattoo on drums, but a tiger rushed out and carried off the last man of the party. Some of the tigers were at length captured in a pitfall, and one was exhibited in the Calcutta Zoological Gardens.

A gallant deed was related in the Report of a Survey Officer in the Sundarbans a few years ago. An Indian surveyor was seated at a table at work when an assistant close to him was seized and carried off by a tiger. Without hesitation the surveyor took his brass sight-ruler, weighing about two pounds, and ran after the tiger. He came up with the beast and beat it over the head with the ruler until it dropped its victim and made off. The man was deservedly promoted for his gallantry, but unfortunately the assistant was killed in the first onslaught.

There are many superstitions relating to the tiger. In the Deccan I found an idea prevalent among my native followers that the aboriginal Gonds had the power of protecting tigers from the hunter by deflecting his bullets, and I was advised in consequence to make friends with the Gond Raja when shooting in his neighbourhood. And each year, in deference to my people, the tiger-hunting expedition in the jungles of the Pein Gunga used to begin with the sacrifice of a goat at the tomb of a Muhammadan saint, Shaikh Farid, near Fort Mahor, both Hindus and Musalmans joining in the rites, and all of us afterwards eating the flesh of the goat. On the way back a foot of the sacrificial animal used to be hung in a little dilapidated hut, on the top of which a ragged pennon fluttered, and within a red-painted stone formed a symbol of the jungle god. Certainly this was followed by success, for invariably the valley below the tomb, and that in which the Hindu shrine was situated, furnished several tigers, while many were brought to bag in the jungles beyond. After each tiger was killed, a similar sacrifice was carried out at the shrine of the local red symbol, a goat being anointed with wine, and its throat cut when it bowed down before the graven image. It must not, however, be supposed that the stone itself was worshipped; it was merely regarded as a symbol of the Spirit of the Wild.

The Gonds averred that the tiger-god, in the form of a great White Tiger, protected them when they invoked its aid in driving off any specially destructive beast of prey, tiger or leopard, and man-eater or cattle-killer. Thus a leopard which had been carrying off children from a village in the Gond Raja's domain was driven away by this protector shortly before my arrival on the scene.

There is a remarkable story illustrating the widely prevalent superstition that a man-eater is accompanied by the spirit of its last victim, which warns it of the presence of danger. A native hunter sat in a tree over the corpse of a man killed by a tiger. The monster approached to renew the feast, whereupon the corpse raised a grisly right arm and pointed to the watcher in the tree, and the tiger retreated. The watcher descended, pegged down the offending hand, and resumed his vigil. Again the tiger came, but the left hand was raised in warning. Once more the shikari got down, pegged down that hand also, and climbed up to his ambush. The monster approached, there was now nothing to warn him, and when he bent down to feed a well-placed bullet ended his evil life.

A curious belief that the man-eating tiger bears a distinctive mark in the form of a cross on the left side of the body, was found by Colonel Ferris to be prevalent in the Sawantwari State in Western India. A tigress with a three-quarter grown cub had killed a number of people, and was said not to eat them, but to pass them over to her cub, on which the natives averred the man-eating mark would be found. When the cub was shot, the man-eating mark was there in the form of a distinct cross. This was in country bordering on Roman Catholic Goa, so the idea may have a religious origin. Markings on tigers vary greatly with the individual, and assume many patterns, and the cross mark was no doubt a coincidence. If the natives had been near enough to see the corpses of the dead dealt with by the tigress and cub, they may have been near enough to see the mark of the cross on the living animal, although Colonel Ferris said that they could not have seen the mark, and they told him of it six weeks before he shot the beast. He afterwards killed the tigress, but does not state whether it bore a cross or not.

CHAPTER X

MORE MAN-EATERS

THE long-established supposition that man-eaters are always mangy or disabled animals has now been dissipated. The general experience of those who have had to deal with them is that they are often young and generally vigorous, although some kind of disablement has sometimes led to this habit. The idea perhaps arose from one or more such instances. It was widely prevalent. In one instance a man-eating tiger was described as having a naked head, " like a great earthware pot," due to the baneful effects of eating human flesh. But whether to beasts of prey or cannibals, human flesh appears to be as nourishing as that of any other creature. A man-eating tiger I met with was as fine a specimen as any seen and shot. The skin is of deep sienna colour, with broad and velvety black stripes; the teeth and claws are in as perfect and unblemished condition to-day as when the animal was killed, more than thirty years ago. Most man-eaters are tigresses; this was a male. It had destroyed a dozen or so people, but was not averse from buffaloes, and had killed one in a wide and bush-filled ravine the night before it was shot. I rode out one morning 65 miles to a village near its haunts, where a famous sportsman, Colonel Nightingale, had killed a man-eating tiger thirty years before.

This tiger gave good sport. Soon after the beat began a tremendous roaring announced his presence. The roars came closer to the slope at the top of which I was posted. The tiger was penned in by the beaters, who crowded round so that the beast was surrounded and had no point of egress. With some difficulty they were got into trees. Suddenly this immense tiger burst from the jungle below and dashed up the hill towards me. I shot him through the body, but he rushed on, and it took two or three more bullets to finish him—a splendid animal with the best skin of any I have shot.

Tigers have long disappeared from the neighbourhood of Bombay, but a stray one was shot on the island of Salsette only some three years ago. Sixty to seventy years ago man-eaters infested that island and the Thana District. Mr. Inverarity, a famous Bombay sportsman, told me of a tiger on Salsette which attacked two men, one of whom went up a tree while the other escaped. The tiger attempted to climb the tree, but could not reach the man, and it then hid in the jungle close by. Poor Pandu, thinking the coast was clear, descended and made tracks for his village, but the tiger seized and ate him. The inquest report stated that "Pandu died of the tiger eating him; there was no other cause of death. Nothing was left except some fingers, which probably belonged to the right or left hand." Perhaps the jury wisely refrained from making a thorough search in the man-eater's haunts, for the tiger usually leaves as much as the dogs left of Jezebel, "the skull, and the feet, and the palms of her hands."

Mr. Mulock, of the Indian Civil Service, killed several man-eating tigers not far from Bombay, one at

Tungar, 35 miles off, which carried off a man when he was close by. He went after it at once and found the half-eaten corpse and shot the tigress, which was the culprit. Another tiger killed a number of people, among others a woman who went into the forest with a companion to gather sticks. They saw the tiger and fled, but it ran after and caught and killed one of them. This open pursuit is rare, for the victim is seized unawares from behind and seldom sees the assailant, while after a failure the attack is not usually renewed, but man-eaters, like other tigers, vary in character. An old tigress was in the habit of seizing her victims unawares; she was about to take a boy one afternoon when he awoke and saw her and she sneaked off. Another was said to remove all the clothes, ornaments, and hair of the corpse before eating it.

The Central Provinces have always been infested by man-eaters, in this respect coming next to Bengal. There have never been many in the Deccan. The prevalence of these destructive beasts in various provinces may be roughly judged from the following human mortality figures for one year: Madras, 83; Bombay, 22; Bengal, 347; North West Provinces and Oudh, 28; Punjab, 2; Central Provinces, 167; British Burma, 16; Mysore and Coorg, 2; Assam, 138; Hyderabad, 11. One tiger destroyed half the population of some small villages up the Pench river 15 miles from Nagpur. Although the tiger, unlike the panther, will not generally enter human habitations, this one was said to be in the habit of "walking through a village in broad daylight, entering house after house when the doors were open, and if the houses were empty and he found no game, he would break all the earthen cooking-pots, and return grumbling fiercely to the jungle."[1] He was shot by a band of native shikaris, who watched for him several days from an ambush in the thatch of a deserted house.

A tigress lived on a wooded spur through which a tunnel had been cut near Darekasa station, where in three years she killed about forty human beings employed on the Bengal-Nagpur railway. With her cubs this tigress used a cave in bamboo and other jungle where there were several springs of water; a stone outside the cave was deeply scored with scratches of their claws. She was hunted by many sportsmen, but was very cunning and never returned to a kill. "At 2.20 on the 24th February, 1889, she jumped down from the top of a slope of a cutting about twelve feet on to the line where a gang of permanent-way men were at work, snatched one of them up, and vanished up the opposite slope in a second. She carried the body to a pool 300 yards off and there ate it."[2] On the 29th she attacked a wood-cutter near the railway, but was driven off by his companion who went for her with an axe. She killed more men during the ensuing hot weather, but her ultimate fate is not recorded.

The Nagpur country always had a bad reputation for man-eating tigers. One was killed near Seoni by a sportsman who was walking through the jungle followed by his gun-bearer when the latter was seized and carried off. He fired and wounded the animal, which dropped its prey and retreated, but the man was already dead with his chest crushed in. The same sportsman shot another man-eater near Nagpur. He had crossed a

[1] *Reminiscences of Sport in India.* By General E. F. Burton.

[2] *Journal of the Bombay Natural History Society*, Vol. IV.

dry watercourse on horseback with his followers behind him, when a shout made him turn and he saw a tiger in the midst of the natives with the dog-boy in its jaws. As it made off with its prey, one of the men fired a gun and the dog-boy staggered back in a few moments but fell and died with his throat torn open. The tiger, an infamous man-eater which had killed scores of people, was followed up and shot.

One of the most amazing encounters with a man-eater was recorded in the *Indian Forester* for July 1889, where the history of the tigress of Mandali was related at length. This tigress ranged the Jumna valley in the neighbourhood of Chakrata, a hill-station in the Himalayas, frequenting a ridge between that river and the Tons from 1876 until her death in 1889, haunting the vicinity of a number of villages and taking to man-eating owing to the scarcity of game and the difficulty of hunting and securing wild animals. The ridge was 10,000 feet above the sea, and was covered with snow in winter, when the tigress retired to lower elevations. She had apparently followed the herds from the Dun forests, and had cubs with her, and had been left behind when the herdsmen took their cattle down at the beginning of winter.

She began man-eating by killing three men in 1880, when her cubs were destroyed, and as time went on her taste for human flesh increased until she came to prefer man to beast, whether wild or domesticated. On one occasion she walked past a cow and calf and took a man sleeping in the same outhouse. Other men, roused by the noise, got up, and went to the door to see what had happened; the tigress dropped her prey and waited near; she returned when the men had gone back, picked up her victim and made off with him. Then, just as he came to, the other men hearing his groans, at last realizing what had happened, rushed out again only in time to see the tigress disappearing with their comrade down the slope on to the road below.

In 1883 an officer was in camp when an orderly in a small tent by a large fire, being a light sleeper, was awakened at midnight by the tread of a heavy animal galloping down the soft slope just above the tent. He snatched a brand from the fire and shouted; just then the flaps of the tent were suddenly flung open, and he saw the man-eater glaring at him with only the log-fire between them. His shout awoke the half-dozen other occupants of the tent, and they made so much noise while he kept flourishing the firebrand across the opening, that the tigress could only stand and glare at them. In two minutes the whole camp was up, and men with sticks, torches, and anything they could pick up, rushed to the scene. The tigress, enraged, backed some paces, tearing up the earth in her rage, and skulked slowly away to cover close by.

On May 7th, 1889, a party of Forest School students encamped at Mandali. The tigress had a few days previously attempted to carry off one of the shepherds, but had been driven off by his father who struck her on the head with a stick while a dog seized her by the neck, and she retreated under these assaults, the shepherd only having his back scratched. She had also proved her exceptional boldness by entering a cabin built of large hewn slabs in which eighteen men were asleep, and carrying off one of the sleepers without disturbing the others. This animal or another had gone up to one of a group of huts 24 miles into the interior from Mandali, after she had killed and eaten two people. She was accompanied by two young cubs, and pushed open the door, entered the hut, stepped over the first sleeper, and seized the next one by the throat, killing him instantly.

On the night of May 11th the man-eater rushed at a herdsman at Mandali but he escaped into his hut, and she then chased and killed one of his young cattle at the head of a ravine; in the morning a postman and syce met and shouted at her. Arrangements were made by Mr. Osmaston, a young Forest Officer, to sit up on a *machan* or platform for the tigress over the dead bullock that evening, May 12th, but at 2 o'clock a man who was watching the kill came to say that he had heard a heavy animal coming down the ravine. Osmaston, taking a 12-bore rifle, and Hansard, a student, then went after the tigress, one walking on each side of the ravine. The ground was rough, and they could move only very slowly. They had gone about 180 yards when the ground became too rough for walking on Osmaston's side, and he descended to the bottom of the ravine, Hansard walking parallel with him about 30 yards off on the steep slope. Osmaston described what followed: "Suddenly I heard a thud, followed by a series of short, snappish, angry growls, and at the same moment I heard groans and cries for help from Hansard, crushed to the ground by the tigress, and struggling, face downward, to get free. The tigress appeared to be tearing his face and neck with her claws. As quickly as I could I levelled the 12-bore at the brute, and, although I was very much afraid of hitting Hansard, I knew it was the poor fellow's last chance. So I pulled the trigger, and to my relief saw the brute relax her hold and come rolling down the precipitous slope, which ended in a 15-foot drop, nearly sheer. The tigress never ceased her hideous growling even to the moment when she fell into the ravine and lay there in the water within a couple of yards of me. I was hemmed in on both sides, so I knew if she was still capable of doing damage it was all up with me. I fired the second barrel into her, and springing down the precipitous ravine, a feat which I don't think I could possibly perform a second time, I rushed up the side of the ravine and made for the place where I had seen Hansard lying, his face all gory and apparently dying. I could not, however, find him, and I rushed back to camp, the direction of which I more or less knew, across several spurs and ravines." Fortunately the prompt and effective action taken by this young and inexperienced officer, who showed a nerve and promptitude beyond all praise, had finished off the tigress and saved his companion who would have been killed had there been a moment's hesitation.

The tigress had sprung on Hansard from behind, bearing him down at once. Happily all but one of her teeth had been reduced to mere stumps, for she was probably not less and perhaps much more than seventeen years old. She could do little more than use her claws, but with time she could even with toothless jaws have crushed his skull to pieces. She clawed his face and back, dislocating the jaw; the only dangerous wound was made by the solitary canine which penetrated behind the ear to the back of the mouth. Fortunately Osmaston had acted immediately and shot her before she could do further damage; his bullet completely disabled the beast by smashing the spine, raking along under it, and blowing up everything in the way until it stopped in the lungs. A minute after the second shot, Osmaston's orderly, who had been at the *machan* built near the dead bullock, hearing his master's cry for help, rushed down the ravine and found the tigress dead and Hansard lying insensible in the water at the bottom of the ravine. After the tigress had let go her hold and rolled down the slope, Hansard, thinking she would come back for him, had crawled down into the ravine, only to find himself within 10 yards of his enemy who was of course already dead. It was lucky that the shot against her spine had made the brute relax her hold at once; otherwise he would have rolled down with her and certainly have been killed by the fall.

The tigress was 8 feet 8 inches in length. Her canines, with one exception, had been worn down to mere stumps. The dead bullock had not a tooth-mark on it; its neck was broken, and little flesh was eaten. The tigress was in miserable condition, having been unable to eat a full meal. Hansard suffered for a long time, the wound behind the ear being deep and poisonous, but he eventually recovered.

There are few instances of Europeans being carried off and eaten by tigers. Besides the Sagar Island case, I can call to mind only one such record, that of a Roman Catholic priest who was killed and devoured some forty years ago by a man-eater in Assam. But Europeans have had narrow escapes. Perhaps the most remarkable was that of a planter in Assam who was sitting in the verandah of his house when a tiger came in, seized him by the hand, and walked off with him, the man having to accompany the beast, walking beside it. Fortunately a friend who was there realized what was happening; he took his rifle, followed the party down the path, and killed the tiger before it had done further harm.

A few years ago Mr. George, District Forest Officer, was walking on a forest road and behind him his Gond Forest Guard, who was carrying his 12-bore gun with the safety-catch down. A tigress seized George by the back of the neck and threw him to the ground. The Gond did not understand the safety-catch, so clubbed the gun and beat the tigress over the head until she let go. She did not renew the attack, and George recovered so far that he was able to walk two miles to his camp, accompanied by the tigress which was unwilling to relinquish her prey, and made demonstrations, but was kept off by the Gond. Fortunately one or more of her canine teeth was missing, or death would probably have been instantaneous. It is satisfactory to know that the Forest Guard was suitably rewarded for his pluck and resource by the award of the Albert Medal and the gift by the Central Provinces Government of a cart and pair of bullocks.

One district of the Central Provinces has long been infested by man-eating tigers, two of which were killed by Lieutenant R. S. Burton, R.A., in 1930. One of them had killed a goat and was shot with the goat's head in his mouth. The day before he made several attempts to take a man from a party of fifty forest workers who were burning undergrowth. When the tiger came, the men got near the fired jungle and shouted, making demonstrations. The tiger roared round them and made three rushes, no doubt trying to frighten and separate them, so that he might seize a straggler. He then walked down the fire-line, from which he was attracted by a bleating goat tethered to a log near the village as bait for a leopard. The tiger dragged away both the goat and the log to which it was attached, and ate the goat. He afterwards killed another goat and was shot as related.

There are still man-eating tigers in the same part of the country. On a day in April 1931 an old man, a middle-aged man, and a boy were sleeping in the open field two miles from any forest. They had been employed in hanging tobacco leaves to dry on the cross-stays of a platform erected on poles, and had no thought of danger, for the area had long been cleared of jungle. These people are careless by nature, unless something happens to affect them personally, when they become extremely cautious. The three lay side by side. In the night the old man was awakened by the sound of the younger man being dragged off by a tiger which had seized him by the back of the neck. With the man's young son he followed the drag, both shouting and beating the ground with sticks, whereupon the tiger dropped its victim, but continued to prowl round the place making demonstrations. The man was dead. They dragged the corpse back to their sleeping place. Fortunately the tiger found a young buffalo wandering not far off, killed and ate it, and went away before dawn.

Lieutenant R. S. Burton was in camp a few miles off when he was told of the tragedy next morning. That night he had the corpse roped to a stake, so that the tiger should not carry it off with a rush, while he lay on the platform close by. As soon as he was left alone, an old jackal appeared and called, and soon a troop of jackals were yelling all round; they attacked the body, eating all the flesh of the face and neck, but leaving the rest; in that great heat the body soon became most unpleasant to the watcher above. The man-eater did not return.

Another man was killed on April 29th, and on May 1st a wood-cutter was taken off the fire-line while cutting wood in the morning. Fire-lines are cleared of forest so as to divide the forest into blocks, thus preventing the spread of fire by confining a conflagration to the block affected. The whole of one thigh of this corpse was eaten, as well as the left leg except ten inches of shin, and the whole of the lower part of the body except the other leg was eaten. The ground was too hard for tracking, so it was not possible to say whether this was the work of a tiger or a tigress. The beast did not return.

Jackals are not infrequently sufferers from hydrophobia, which spreads from them to the village dogs. Some years ago Captains Farley and Parker were in camp at Christmas time. They went to sleep at midnight, Farley having his two fox-terriers sleeping on the end of his camp-bed. At four o'clock in the morning he was awakened by a frightful commotion, and found Parker on all-fours in a state of collapse with blood streaming from his nose. He said he had been pulled out of bed by the nose by some animal. The dogs had slept throughout. Farley heated some water and dressed the nose which was badly lacerated, using permanganate of potash as an antiseptic, and they turned in again. After breakfast a Baluchi who had been sleeping not far off came with his nose in a still more lacerated state than Parker's. He said that he had been attacked by a wolf and that a boy had been bitten the day before. It is more probable that the assailant was a mad jackal.

Parker was sent off to the Pasteur Institute at Paris, as there were no such places in India in those days, although one was soon afterwards established at Kasauli. It was feared that, being bitten so dangerously near the brain, he would arrive too late for effective treatment, but he suffered no ill effects, although both the Baluchi and the boy died soon afterwards from hydrophobia. The incident shows that the dangers of camp-life are not confined to attacks by tigers and leopards.

It has already been said that onslaughts by tigers on human beings are usually made from behind, at any rate in daylight, while the idea that the human eye will avert attack has often been referred to. Attacks from behind were always made by a man-eater which was in the habit of haunting a road through a forest in the Central Provinces, and taking the drivers out of passing bullock-carts. All cases of men being killed by wild animals had to be reported to the police, and the corpse left *in situ* until they arrived on the scene; otherwise people might conveniently murder their enemies and ascribe the fatality to the man-eater.

At nine o'clock one morning a cart drawn by a pair of bullocks was rumbling along the road, the driver seated on the single pole that supported the yoke resting on the necks of the hump-backed animals, occasionally twisting their tails between his toes, or with objurgations beating them with his short-handled, leather-thonged whip. All unconscious of danger, he did not see the monster which slunk along with velvet footfall under cover by the roadside, awaiting a favourable opportunity to seize her prey; others might have been taken before, but the man was a fatalist like all his kind, and gave no thought to a danger that had not hitherto come within his personal experience. He exchanged greetings with another cartman who passed him, but the tigress had already selected her victim. And now no one else was in sight. The moment had come. Unobserved, her coat shining like molten gold in the light of the sun, she rushed silently from the cover of the bushes and bamboo clumps that fringed the roadside, and in a moment leapt upon her prey, seized him by the back of the neck, pulled him from his perch, and made off through the forest, trailing her ghastly burden whose feet dragged along the ground. No sound escaped him; his breath was stifled before he could cry out, and in an instant his life was spent.

The terrified bullocks careered madly ahead until a few hundred yards further on they came to a stop before some forest workers who turned them back to look for the driver, who they supposed must have fallen from his seat or got down for some purpose and so allowed the animals to make off. They came to the scene of the tragedy, and were horror-struck to see the tracks of the monster and the trail of the dragging heels of her victim. Fearful to follow, and unarmed against so terrible a beast, they drove the cart back a few miles to the police-station, and gave notice of what they had seen.

It was midday by the time the Inspector of Police set out for the scene of the tragedy, accompanied by a constable and some of the bolder villagers. On the way they were met with the news that a second man had been taken by a tiger not far from the spot where the first kill took place. This was strange. Were there two man-eaters? For the tigress was always satisfied with one victim to provide food for a day or two. They came to the spot where the first man had been killed. They took up the trail, and arrived on the brink of a ravine with steep banks. On the other side of the ravine, with its back leaning against the perpendicular bank, the corpse of the victim faced them, sitting propped up, with staring eyes bulging from their sockets. No tiger was in view. But tracks led to and fro, to and fro, upon the sandy soil, clearly imprinted where it could be seen that the tigress had paced backwards and forwards many times, watching but fearing to approach the dead eyes that glared upon her from their sockets. She had dropped the corpse in climbing the steep bank, and it had sat down in such a position that she could not approach to seize it from behind, while she was fearful of even unseeing eyes that now at last looked upon the face of death. So she had paced to and fro for a time and then, urged by hunger, sought another victim, whose body was found almost all eaten.

This incident is certainly significant of the theory that the human eye will avert the attack of a man-eating wild beast; but it has no effect in stopping the charge of an animal, rendered ferocious by wounds, and determined to avenge itself upon its enemy or to defend itself against further injury. It may, however, merely indicate that the habit of seizing its victim unawares is so ingrained in the nature of the beast of prey that it will not attack where it is aware of being observed.

While few who have been seized by a tiger survive

the terrific onslaught, the power of the jaws, and the poisonous deposit on the teeth and claws which causes blood-poisoning, some have recovered entirely and some, like the late Sir Edward Braddon, with the loss of a limb. Mr. Inverarity saw a man who had been seized by a man-eating tiger by the nape of the neck; he recovered. He was the last of a single file of villagers, and on the tiger seizing him, the others turned and drove it off. He was insensible and when he came to had no idea of what had happened to him. So it seems probable that animals killed usually suffer but little.

Herdsmen and other unarmed natives often display remarkable courage. Sterndale in his *Natural History* relates that on one occasion one of a herd of cattle, attacked close to his camp, was rescued single-handed by its owner, who laid his heavy iron-bound staff across the tiger's back; and when he rushed out to see what was the matter, he found the man coolly dressing the wounds of his cow, muttering to himself: "The robber! My last cow, and I had five of them!" He did not seem to think he had done anything wonderful, and was surprised that it should be supposed he would let his last heifer go the way of all the others. In the case of an attack on a herdsman by a man-eater, piercing cries of "Tiger! Tiger!" were heard, and a struggle was going on in the bush. The buffaloes threw up their heads and grunting loudly charged down on the spot and then went charging on through the brushwood. The herdsman was badly scratched, but escaped any serious fang-wounds from his having seen the tiger coming at him, and stuffed his blanket into its open mouth, while he belaboured it with his axe. But for his buffaloes he would have been a dead man. I saw a man save himself from the attack of a leopard, which I afterwards shot, by " feeding " it in the same manner with his shoulder-cloth.

Tigers are not always courageous ; even village boys have been known to turn a tiger out of quarters they thought too close, and pelt him with stones. But the wounded tiger is terrible in attack. In 1888 in the Melghat Forest a wounded tiger was being followed by a Police Officer, Mr. Cuthbert Fraser, when it charged, seized the constable who was with him, and bit off the top of his head just as one " tops " a boiled egg. The man was found dead in a sitting position. The smashing blow with the paw we often read about seldom occurs ; in the case of two men killed by the same tiger, Sterndale mentions that one had his skull fractured by a blow, and the other was seized by the loins and died immediately.

One of the most dramatic accounts of the death of a man-eater is given in his *Wild Sports of India* by Captain Shakespear, who killed an infamous tiger when he was on the march in the Raipur District in 1856. Hearing of this animal, he turned aside from his route and encamped at a village which was deserted except by one small family, owing to the man-eater's depredations. Here a pair of tigers lived on a lofty and rocky hill, from which they descended at night to pull people out of their huts. Shakespear describes how he shot the tiger at dawn on the carcass of a white calf which it had struck down, and how, when it was wounded by his first bullet: " Immediately the tiger sprang to his feet and exposed his broad left side, I stepped from behind the tree, looked at him in the face with contempt, as if he had been a sheep, and while he passed me with every hair set, his beautiful white beard and whiskers spread, and his eye like fire, with the left barrel I shot him through the heart. He went straight on with undiminished speed, each bound covering 15 feet at least, for 25 yards, and fell on his head under the lowest rock of the mountain on which was his stronghold." The gallant captain was fortunate, for a wounded tiger in such circumstances follows its nose, and had that been directed towards the sportsman, not even the contemptuous look, nor the supposed power of the human eye would have saved him in the final rush, though the tiger was shot through the heart. A wounded tiger is anything but a sheep! Thirteen quarts of fat were taken from this tiger, and when the renter of the village came to beg a pipkin full, Shakespear said to him, "Of course, it is the fat of your own villagers!" The man smiled a ghastly smile; it was too true to be a joke; and the remembrance too recent to be relished.

There was still the tigress. That night Shakespear had all the camp-fires lit and the sentries posted. At ten o'clock he was awakened by a shout that one of his troopers had been carried off by a tiger. It was pitch-dark and the fires were out except some embers near which the trooper was seized and over which the tigress had sprung on him. She had seized him by the head as he was preparing to go on duty. A ravine led towards the mountain, and Shakespear and his men followed up this, shouting the trooper's name. He had at first fired off his rifle. Nothing was to be seen, and nothing heard but a sigh, until later on when monkeys chattered in the trees and the crunching of the trooper's bones horrified the listeners. They had passed in the night within 15 yards of the body, which was found in the morning with one leg eaten off up to the knee. Shakespear sat over a calf that evening and had a shot at the tigress, which he thought was wounded, but she was not seen again.

Tigers have their place in military history. In the Mahratta War of 1817, man-eaters took their toll of stragglers of the Deccan Army under Sir Thomas Hislop as it marched through the valley of the Tapti river on the way to Mehidpur, just as Herodotus relates that the lions of the Macedonian mountains harried the baggage-camels of Xerxes. After the dispersal of the Pindaris in 1819 at the end of the war, their famous leader, Chithu, deserted by all his followers, at last wandered off alone in the jungles on the banks of the Tapti near Asirgarh, where he was killed and devoured by a man-eating tiger, the remains being recognised by the discovery of the victim's head.

One of the most terrible man-eaters was the tigress destroyed by Sanderson, the history of which is related with graphic realism in his book, *Thirteen Years Among the Wild Beasts of India*. This was in Mysore, where man-eaters are rare. Among the victims of this brute was the priest of a small jungle temple, to which he was on his way one morning when the tigress with her cub suddenly stepped into the path. The bullock the holy man was riding took fright, dismounted his rider, and galloped off to the village, while the priest was killed and eaten in an adjacent ravine. In the same neighbourhood the next victim was a herdsman who was thrown up into a thicket several feet off the ground by the attack, and there left caught in thorny creepers.

He was not found until next morning, when he was still alive, hanging mangled and moaning, head downwards in the thicket. He died soon after being taken down.

Tigers made their way to Singapore in the early part of the last century, and by 1848 had greatly increased in numbers. The loss of life from their depredations in that year was supposed to amount to at least 200 grown persons, and a gentleman who made enquiries found that nearly 300 human beings had been carried off in one year, of whom only seven had been reported to the police. Efforts were made to destroy the tigers, and five were captured in pitfalls in one quarter. They must have been scarce a few years before, when even the natives did not know of their occurrence.

How did they reach the island? One may have been accidentally carried across the narrow strait which separates it from the mainland, and its cry in the pairing season may have induced another to follow, and, finding abundance of food, they increased and multiplied. This is a more rational mode of accounting for their presence than to suppose that they chased their prey over, for it is contrary to the nature of the beast to follow in pursuit after a first unsuccessful attempt.

A. R. Wallace, writing in 1854, described the island as a multitude of small hills, three or four hundred feet high, the summits of many still covered with virgin forest, frequented by wood-cutters. Here and there were tiger pits, carefully covered over with leaves and sticks, and so well concealed that he narrowly escaped falling into one. They were shaped like an iron furnace, wider at the bottom than the top, and 15 or 20 feet deep. Formerly a sharp stake was stuck erect in the bottom, but after a traveller had been killed by falling on one, its use was forbidden. He said that there were always a few tigers roaming about, and that they killed on an average a Chinaman every day, principally those working in the gambir plantations, which were always made in newly cleared jungle.

It was related a few years ago that a small boy living in the district found a nice kitten in the jungle and began playing with it. His father, who was gathering firewood, saw that the supposed kitten was a tiger-cub, whereupon the boy took up a piece of wood and killed it. The father, fearing that the tigress would come, got the boy up a tree, tied him there and climbed up himself. The tigress came and, seeing the dead cub and the people in the tree, tried to spring at them. The man struck it with his heavy hunting knife, and so disabled it that it lay down and soon died.

CHAPTER XI

THE TIGER OF THE TEMPLE

MANY strange and unaccountable things happen in the jungle, as we may learn from the aboriginal inhabitants who share its fastnesses with the wild beasts, and are acquainted with unimagined forces and mysteries of Nature. What, indeed, do we really know of the ways and the senses of the wild? Too often human processes of thought are attributed to wild beasts, yet we do not know what faculties they possess. How can we account for the power of certain female moths to attract from a distance the males of their species; the sudden change of direction in full flight of a pack of wild duck; the instantaneous and universal cessation of the screech of cicadas that fills a vast forest and is as suddenly resumed; the sudden rise of fish in every part of a river or lake, and their simultaneous retirement to the depths? Have animals methods of communication, psychological or otherwise, that are absent or latent in man? Spiritualists ascribe powers of communication between the living and those who have passed beyond the life of the world; can animals communicate in the same way?

The jungle men are in close communication with the spirit of the wild, represented by the symbolical red-painted stone that is to be found beneath a sacred tree in every valley. And they hold that the spirit of a human being killed by a man-eater accompanies its destroyer to give warning to the monster of impending danger. To the Gonds themselves my shikaris ascribed power to protect tigers by turning aside the bullets of the hunter. It is well to propitiate the wild men if one wishes to deal with the wild beasts! But these people are very timid and reticent.

My camp was pitched on the bank of a river, now nearly dry, on the edge of a forest abounding in game. In the hills behind the tents, some four miles off, were cool and shady valleys and nullahs, haunts suitable for tigers impatient of the heat, where they could find shade and water even at the hottest season of the year as well as plenty of game and, in the more open jungle, herds of cattle. The reticence of the people is intelligible. For many centuries they were oppressed, and are naturally nearly as shy as the wild animals of the fastnesses into which they were driven by invading hordes before the dawn of history. Even then they were not safe from molestation in their remote jungles, and suffered much before the establishment of English rule. Armies marched through their country from Northern India to the South, while marauding bands of Pindari robbers traversed the passes of the Satpura Hills and did not spare the jungle tribes. Where these tribes once dwelt in fertile valleys they had been dispossessed by Hindus and driven farther into remoter hills and jungles whose principal inhabitants are predaceous animals. In the mountains south of the Tapti river is a stream called the River of Blood, the scene of the massacre of a whole tribe of aborigines by a band of Arabs in the service of a Mahratta chief. Now they no longer fear man, for English rule has not only delivered them from organized hordes of robbers, but protects them from the oppression which would be their lot if that rule were withdrawn. But they are shy and retiring, and they fear the powers of Nature and the wrath of their animist gods, among whom the tiger occupies the first place.

There were vague and indefinite rumours of the presence of a man-eating tiger in the forest, and my camp servants showed some alarm. Some said that many people had been killed, but that the man-eater had gone away. There had been no recent deaths, and the jungle had been free for some months, but the Gonds would tell nothing and would not give the beast a name. There were certainly plenty of tigers in the valleys among the hills. We found fresh tracks of a very big male and older marks of others, and we picketed out buffaloes in hopes of getting a kill that night. We were not disappointed. On visiting the place next morning we saw a crow perched on a branch over a pool of water, cawing vociferously, and there were vultures in the trees. We did not go near for fear of disturbing the tiger, who should by now have taken up his place of rest for the day. But we viewed the kill from a distance, and then went on up the valley to look at the other buffaloes, none of which had been taken.

On our return, tracks showed that the big tiger had followed us up the valley for a long way; it looked as though the hunter had been hunted, but perhaps the beast only wished to see us safely off the premises. But my men insisted that it was the man-eater. They naturally would, although my view was that it was a mere tradition of long ago. Tales of these monsters persist for many years, and are sometimes told as though they were the happenings of yesterday. The tiger had turned off from our tracks into the upper part of the nullah, and we hoped had gone back to the kill.

We returned to camp and beaters were collected, but only from the village at the foot of the hills; the Gonds would not come; they made many excuses; they had work to do; they had to gather the blossoms of the mohwa; they gave any excuse they could think of. But there were enough without them. At two o'clock, after arranging the beat, I took up my position in a tree overlooking the nullah, a couple of hundred yards below the pool. At the first shout of the beaters the tiger roared, and shortly afterwards he roared repeatedly and angrily; but soon he came slowly forth; a bullet behind the shoulder dropped him dead on the spot. He was a huge beast, heavy and fat. My old shikari, Nathu, during the process recounted how he had faced the tiger when it roared and tried to break out of the beat, but he had turned it back with a shout and a flourish of his spear, which I can well believe, for he was not only truthful but a rash and fearless man. He would rush up to a wounded beast, tiger or leopard, and belabour it with stick and tongue, when the beast was far enough gone to be unable to retaliate. We skinned the tiger on the spot, for it was far from camp, and left the carcass to the vultures, which soon picked all the flesh off the bones.

Perhaps it would have been wise to remove or bury the bones, for a day or two afterwards another tiger killed a buffalo picketed by the same pool. But he ate none of it, and his tracks in the sandy bed of the nullah showed that he had fled the spot at once. My shikaris said that he had been warned off the kill by the ghost of his predecessor; but it was more likely that he had recognised his relative's bones which lay bleaching in the sun. Still, it seemed uncanny when two nights afterwards, the carcass of the last buffalo having been removed, and a fresh one tied up in its place, a tigress with two cubs passed close by and did not even kill, although the tell-tale tracks showed where they had stopped to inspect the feast provided for them. Perhaps they did not like the look of a tethered buffalo, or preferred venison. At any rate, like the last tiger, they fled into the night.

I resolved to make another attempt, and took up a concealed position next evening in a banyan tree above the pool, where there was a view of the patient beast chewing the cud. Already the sun had sunk to a spear's length above the hills in the west, and as night's phantom army, the shadows of the forest, advanced across the water, animals came down to drink. A herd of spotted deer paused for a while upon the brink, a little four-horned antelope came on dainty feet, and dipped his muzzle in the pool; a jungle-cock crowed loudly and repeatedly in a patch of grass, and his challenge was taken up from an adjacent thicket.

In the tropics night falls with sudden swiftness; the sun drops down into the deeps behind the mountains; birds and animals that have been to drink disappear, and in a moment all is plunged in darkness; the stars throw down their spears; the voices of the forest are hushed, and the beasts of the night begin to prowl; there is a mysterious silence broken only sometimes by a voice of fear. There was to be a long wait until the moon rose at midnight, and even if the tiger came now it could be seen no more than the patient buffalo that stood below in happy ignorance of impending fate. After a long day in the heat of the sun, the watcher over the pool is likely to doze off to sleep, trusting to awake when the moon rises to light up whatever may be seen beneath.

Breaking the silence of the forest there came a cry of human agony, then for a moment all was still. It was like broad daylight; the heavy breathing of a tiger, and his velvet footfall on the dry leaves came up the nullah; I could see but could not move; the heavy tread came nearer, with the trail of dragging heels along the ground, and the laboured breathing of the beast as he approached the pool with his prey in his jaws. He passed beneath my tree, but even though bright moonlight turned night into day, so bright that one might have read a book, no tiger could be seen. He dropped his burden by the water's edge, and there came the lap, lapping of his tongue, which sent rings out in ripples from the margin of the pool. Then there was the sound of jaws closing again on the neck of the prey, and of the heavy tread as he passed on up the nullah, unseen but heard, the great paws printing off their tracks one by one in the sand, and the trail of the dragging feet beside them. And so " It " passed, and with it the strong smell of wild beast. A hot wind stirred among the drying leaves of the branches that had been cut to furnish my ambush. The moon had risen high in the heavens, and looked down on the patient buffalo, standing in the moonlight chewing the cud on the margin of the pool. But no tiger came to kill him.

At daybreak my men were on the scene. We went

up the nullah, following the tracks of a tiger that had passed by in the night, over the old footmarks of the tigress and her cubs, and those of deer and other animals. As we followed the course of the nullah, now dry after many months of drought, something gleamed white beneath a bush in the rays of the risen sun. It was a human skull. Here we lost the tiger's tracks. We returned down the nullah in the direction from which the animal had come, and on the bank there lay a woodman's rusty axe, which, like the skull, must have lain for many months. I told my shikari of what I had heard and seen, and asked him what he thought of it. "Sahib," he said, "many things happen in the forest. The Gonds could tell us if they would; but they are as wild as the jungle beasts. They say that they will not go into that part of the forest for there is a demon there. They will not tell of what they know, or mention the demon beast, for they fear its vengeance."

I sent for Indru Gond, who came that evening as I sat outside my tent. He was living in a neighbouring hamlet such as are scattered amid the wilderness of forest and mountain, where he and his tribesmen wrested a precarious living from the products of the jungle and the produce of the chase. Where water is scarce in distribution and scanty in supply in the hot weather, they often change their dwelling-places with the seasons, as indicated by the numerous deserted villages. They do well when the mohwa tree furnishes a good crop, which they share with the bears and other animals that feed on the fleshy blossoms as they fall. And when there is a general seeding of bamboos, said to occur only every thirty years, the seed takes the place of rice or other grain.

In this region the higher uplands are for the greater part destitute of water in the hot weather, but in the rainy season abundant grass affords unlimited grazing for the cattle of the Brinjaras, these nomadic people taking up a temporary abode where they can feed their herds. But in summer the hills are burnt and bare; no refreshing streams pour down the burning rocks; no green relieves the arid waste, and both man and beast flee to the lower valleys where there is water to quench their thirst and fodder for their cattle. Thither the attendant tigers follow them to wooded plains, shady valleys, the beds of rivers, nullahs, and cool ravines.

From my tent could be seen both near and more distant hills, and on the summit of one a white speck, a Hindu shrine revealed by the glasses stood out conspicuously. Indru came with his axe, and over his shoulder the broad-bladed, heavy spear, used in hunting pigs, which now stands in a corner of my library, having been bought for two rupees. He squatted in front of me and drank a tot of rum, and I showed him the axe which had some notches cut in the wooden handle, and asked him whose it was. " That belonged to Lungota Pappa," he said, " he went into the forest to cut wood one day last year, and was never seen again." When asked what had happened to Lungota, he replied that no one knew; they had looked for him but could not find him; perhaps a demon had destroyed him.

I pointed to the shrine gleaming white upon the distant hill, and asked him if anyone was living there, and whether we might not find some wild beasts in that likely-looking jungle, which extended up the mountain from the nullah where I had passed the night.

" Sahib ! " he said, " it is an evil spot ; see, even now the temple is as red as the blood of the priest who was killed there ! " And indeed, as we looked, the shrine was crimsoned by the rays of the setting sun. " As for wild beasts," added Indru, " that is the haunt of the tiger who killed and devoured the priest ; but we hope that you shot the demon in the first beat in the nullah, in which my people would not take part ; they were afraid." " And is no one there now ? " I asked. " No one except the spirit of the tiger's victim." The old man paused and looked out towards the shrine, now scarcely visible in the fading light.

" Yes," he resumed, " there is the evil tiger, and there are deer too, and sometimes a herd of bison. The tiger comes to look for us, and he takes Brinjara cattle. The tiger first appeared in the rainy season, when he began killing the cattle, and then he seized several Gonds and Brinjaras. He lurked in the dark places of the jungle, hiding in ambush to seize people when they were chopping wood, or seeking the seeds and fruit which form much of our food. He crept round the outskirts of the villages that lie on the fringe of the forest, or in its shadowy depths, and waylaid the herdsmen as they wended their way homewards at the setting of the sun, when the great grey buffaloes and the lean red and white kine toiled up the dusty path towards the hamlet. He devoured my son !

" It happened one spring morning that we were out under the mohwa tree gathering the fresh blossoms that had fallen during the night, which furnish us with both food and drink. My eldest boy, a fine lad of twelve, wandered a little way into the jungle ; he should have been the support of my old age. Suddenly he screamed one choking cry, and we saw the great yellow beast carrying him off in its jaws, and we all fled. What could we do, an old man, a woman, and three children? Armed only with our axes, how could we hope to rescue the child? Moreover, his cries had already been silenced by death, and we knew that the monster was even now lapping his blood. We went back to the village and raised the alarm. I took my spear and others joined me. We followed on the tracks, beating drums and shouting, and the tiger slunk off, leaving the few fragments of his victim. This was only one among many. Others mourned the loss of friends and relatives. No one was safe. The beast lurked in every thicket, and slew and dragged away his victims in broad daylight, and often devoured them within hearing."

This was Indru's own tale. And later he told me of the death of the priest. The Gonds invoked the aid of their gods without success. In vain they sacrificed a bullock to the Tiger-god, and marched round their village in procession, and took their simple gifts to the red-painted stone that stood beneath the great banyan tree in the valley. Had they offended the Spirit of the Forest? They would see what the Hindu priest who dwelt at the shrine upon the mountain-top could do, taking with them gifts and a goat for sacrifice.

The chief scene of the monster's depredations was a long, broad valley, down one side of which a stream had worn for itself a bed in the rocky soil. On either side rose rugged hills, dark with jungle and seared by rushing torrents which in the rainy season had poured down through deep ravines to the wooded banks of the main watercourse. And in the temple, sole human denizen of the hill, an aged priest, smeared with wood ashes and bowed with the weight of years, tended in solitude his images of stone, and offered frequent orisons to his deities.

For this abode of sanctity a deputation started one morning, taking goat and gifts. It was a long, long tramp up the valley through the jungle to the mountain-top, longer still with the ever-present dread of the lurking terror whose tracks marked the way; and a stiff climb up the path which, worn by the feet of generations of pilgrims who were now as the dust they trod, wound its way over the rocks and through the dense jungle to the temple. When the Gonds reached the summit of the mountain, the sun was just rising over the distant purple hills. As they approached the shrine where the old priest lived, a crow, perched on the stone wall above, cawed loudly and repeatedly. From the dense undergrowth near the spring whose pure water welled from the mountain-side, a gorgeous peacock rose, uttering the trumpet-note of alarm. As they looked for the cause of the disturbance, some living Thing for an instant gleamed golden in the sunlight on the edge of the hill, but no Shape could be distinguished.

A few moments later a sambar stag belled loudly on the hill-side, and the note of alarm was taken up by the spotted deer upon the margin of the stream below. Surely some beast of prey had descended from the hill to the valley beneath! And now in the sky above appeared a few dark specks, soon joined by others, wheeling and circling overhead; vultures which, gathering from afar with unerring instinct, had already viewed a feast. The presence of death seemed to pervade the place, and there could be no doubt that the Thing which for a moment gleamed golden in the sunlight was a beast of prey. A deathlike silence prevailed. A tiny lizard stirring among dry leaves startled the intruders. The Gonds proceeded to the temple, calling on the name of the priest, Indru leading the sacrificial goat which bleated plaintively as though aware of impending doom. Where is the priest ? The terrified Gonds gazed in horror. There had already been a sacrifice. The idol was red with blood. The ghastly head of the old priest, from which the eyes had been plucked by crows, lay on the threshold before his graven images. A few other fragments were scattered about. The hands lay with yellow palms upturned to heaven as though in mute appeal for vengeance. The man-eater had been at work. The old priest had muttered his final prayer, and had been slain on the altar in the very midst of his gods.

CHAPTER XII

THE LEOPARD

THE leopard or panther is perhaps the worst of feline man-eaters, although the mortality bill displays more human victims of the tiger. For example, the statistics of deaths from wild animals in British India in one year show 816 persons killed by tigers and 300 by leopards, Bengal, the greatest sufferer, having a loss of 347 and 149 respectively. But as the deaths from unspecified wild animals in the same year numbered 1323, it is probable that the latter figure includes many due to tigers and leopards. As a man-eater the leopard is probably more frequent. It is more numerous, inhabiting tracts of country that do not afford cover for tigers ; it has a habit of haunting the immediate neighbourhood of villages, where any leopard will take a child if opportunity offers ; it preys especially on the weak, the women and children, and its habits make it more familiar with the presence of man, inducing it to enter huts and compounds where a man-eating tiger rarely ventures.

Earlier sportsmen and naturalists considered that there were two species of this animal, which they termed respectively the panther and leopard, the former being the larger, and this belief still lingers. Perhaps nomenclature had something to do with this confusion, for the same animal used generally to be called leopard in Northern India and panther farther south. There are also other distinct species, the snow leopard or ounce, and the hunting leopard, commonly known as the cheetah, a word that merely means "spotted animal." These two animals, however, do not come within the scope of this work, for neither of them preys on man; they are mild and harmless creatures.

The differences or variations which led to a distinction being made between the so-called panther and leopard relate to size, shape of skull, and texture of fur and coloration. To these some have added a difference in habits and even in temper, the smaller animal often being cited as the fiercer. It is natural that an animal inhabiting the length and breadth of Africa and Asia, under highly variable conditions of climate and habitat, should present considerable varieties in physical characters and in habits. The larger animal has brighter and smoother fur; the skull is more elongated and has a pronounced occipital ridge, the smaller leopard having a rounder skull and no occipital ridge, while its coat is rougher and the fur is more fulvous and not so golden. Allowing for local variation due to environment, these differences can all be referred to age. The young animal has naturally less pigmentation; its skull is rounder, and the pronounced occipital ridge is not yet developed; as in all animals, the coat is rougher—the same thing may be observed in tiger-cubs. In fact, what used to be called the leopard is merely an immature specimen that develops into the mature panther. They are one and the same animal. We might separate mature and immature tigers into different species on practically the same grounds.

The smaller and lighter animals are naturally more

addicted to arboreal habits, whether their size is due to age or individual development; relative character is individual, and there are no grounds for supposing that the smaller is the fiercer of the two. In colder climates thicker and longer fur and an under-pelage may be expected. There is great difference in size between the sexes, the male being much the larger, as in the tiger. The average length of males is about seven feet, and of females a foot less.

It is curious that melanism, so rare in the tiger, should be so common in the leopard. Only one authentic specimen of a black tiger is recorded, but black leopards are common in Malaya and Java, and not uncommon in Canara and other parts of India. There are black leopards in Africa, and black jaguars on the Amazons. In these specimens the rosettes can be seen when looked for in a favourable light. These black animals are freaks, and black and fulvous cubs have been found in one litter. In one case there were one black and three fulvous cubs, both the parents being of the ordinary colour. It is recorded in the *Observer* of January 11th, 1811, that "a large black tiger, the only one ever seen alive in Europe, intended as a present from the King of Java to Bonaparte, taken in the *Gude Vrow* on the passage to France, is now to be seen at Kendrick's Collection of Rare Foreign Beasts and Birds, No. 40, opposite St. James's Church, Piccadilly." This was probably a leopard. But it was not the first, for according to Thomas Pennant, Warren Hastings presented a black leopard, taken in the Sundarbans, to the menagerie in the Tower of London. Pennant also mentions a leopard of a dirty white colour, spotted with grey, taken near Agra and presented to the Emperor Jehangir. White tigers are found, especially on the Upper Narbada in Rewah State, but this is the only known example of a "white" leopard.

Leopards inhabit most varied country, from dense forests to rocky hills with bush-covered sides or thickets in valleys and nullahs. They are often found in bushy wasteland in the midst of tracts of cultivation. Although they drink daily, they do not appear to be as impatient of thirst as the tiger, and they may be found in waterless ravines, while they do not swim or take to water as readily as the tiger, which is so partial to the bath. Like the tiger, the leopard in India is thought to possess no strong sense of smell, and to hunt mainly if not entirely by sight and sound. It is quick to perceive a moving object, but its sight is not otherwise keen. It seizes generally by the throat, much as the tiger attacks its prey, and usually drags the carcass into a thicket or covers it up with dry leaves to hide it from the vultures, or sometimes places it in the fork of a tree at a considerable height from the ground. The remains of human beings, spotted deer, antelope, and pig have been found thus hung in a leopard's tree-larder. Its prey consists mainly of small animals, deer, antelope, pig, monkeys, dogs, and goats, but it will kill larger beasts, cattle, ponies, and donkeys. Hares and rats, porcupines, peafowl, and even scorpions and other insects may be added to the diet.

A leopard will chase and seize monkeys in trees. A Brinjara told me of a peculiar method the leopard has of walking on moonlight nights under the trees where monkeys roost and where their shadows are reflected on the ground. The leopard selects the reflection of the monkey he prefers, perhaps on account of its fatness, and pounces upon it, whereupon the owner of the shadow who is sitting up aloft falls to the ground, an easy prey to the prowler below who, wiser than man, grasps at the shadow and seizes the substance. The truth of this picturesque story cannot be vouched for!

While the leopard is in some respects bold and enterprising, it is generally sneaking and timid. A hyena will drive it from its kill; a pony will keep it off with its heels and a young buffalo with its horns. A party of wild dogs will dispossess it of its prey, and chase it away, and tree it as a dog does a cat. In the Melghat Forest in Berar two leopards were found treed, with a large pack of wild dogs sitting and moving about below. The upper leopard rested on a branch, and the lower one held on perpendicularly. The lower one was seen to jump, and fled, pursued by the pack; the other was shot dead and stuck in a fork of the tree, whereupon some of the dogs came back and could be seen standing on their hind-legs licking the blood as it streamed from the carcass. It is related that the skeleton of a leopard was found in a tree with that of a wild dog impaled on a splintered branch below. It had taken refuge from its enemies, and one of them, jumping up, was transfixed, the leopard dying rather than attempt to descend in the presence of the dog. Leopards have been found dead pierced with porcupine quills, and these are often embedded in the paws.

Leopards will enter a village, a hut, or a tent in search of prey, and especially to seize dogs, which form a favourite food. Sometimes a village is empty of pariah dogs, all having been carried off by the local leopard, but the culprit will not be mentioned by name lest it should take vengeance on its betrayer. They are timid in seizing their prey and are seldom seen in the act. They frequently take dogs which are in company of their masters, especially in the hills, but generally only when the dog has loitered behind or gone into cover by the roadside, so the tragedy is not usually discovered until the dog is missed. A good dog, such as a bull-terrier, will attack and put a leopard to flight, just as old Sal went after the Jalna tiger. A remarkable encounter of this kind is described in *Game and Gun*, March 1931. Dogs should be protected by metal collars well furnished with spikes as a protection against leopards, which have often been foiled by this means when attempting to seize a dog by the throat. They are not safe from attack even when tethered to one's bed; a leopard will drink at night from a basin of water standing near the tent.

There are several methods of hunting the leopard, which affords good sport and is sufficiently formidable to be classed as very dangerous game. They may be met with by chance, perhaps sitting by the roadside or prowling in the jungle in search of prey, but they are elusive and difficult to see. No doubt the sportsman often passes close to a leopard without perceiving it, for it will hide in cover that would scarcely seem to afford concealment for a hare, while its coloration blends wonderfully with the usual environment, especially in the chequered light and shade of bushes in the sunlight, which appears on the ground like the ocellated coat of the animal. I have almost trodden on one which lay under a bush at my feet, but its presence was betrayed by its strong smell.

In many parts of the country leopards inhabit dense forests; in other localities they live in caves and lie up among rocky hills such as are characteristic of the country round Secunderabad. In such places they cannot be driven out, for if they are moved it is merely to creep from one cave or recess to another, while in extensive forest they are difficult to locate. The only way then is to sit up over a goat or dog, or the animal's kill, or over a pool of water at which it may drink, probably at sunset. One may sit in an ambush constructed in a tree, or on the ground, or in a hole with a suitable covering of branches and an aperture to shoot through. If a hole in the ground is well placed, a view of the animal may be obtained, even on a dark night, against the skyline. Or the kill or bait may be illuminated with a lantern or a ray cast through a hole in the side of an eartherware pot containing a light. Then there are possibilities with electric lighting. In most localities the vigil is a dull one, apart from the expectation of the game appearing on the scene. I abandoned it after many weary watches and few successes.

On one occasion I tied up a goat and sat in a tree an hour before sunset and had no sooner climbed up than the leopard, which had been killing calves in the vicinity, bounced out of the bushes close by and seized the goat by the throat. A shot ended the marauder's existence, but too late, for already the life-blood was ebbing from the fang-holes in the gullet of the unfortunate victim, who died to save others. There were many more such incidents; two killed with buckshot at short range, and one, met with by chance, hounded out and shot with a charge of small shot. In a forest abounding with wild life there is a great charm in sitting concealed over a pool of water where the voices of the jungle awake the woodland echoes towards eventide, and where one can watch the birds and beasts that come down to drink. Peafowl, jungle-fowl and painted quail patter over the dry leaves, in which even the stirring of a lizard strikes loudly upon the listening ear. Then little barking deer and four-horned antelope step fearfully to the water's edge, and black-faced monkeys swing down from the branches of the trees and slake their thirst after many a fearful glance around. They have need to be cautious, for the leopard approaches on velvet footfall, and all other animals disappear silently as he pauses for an instant before coming to the pool. Only the monkeys chatter overhead. And if one stays all night, sleep may close the eyes, but the crashing of an approaching bison will rouse from the deepest slumber, and bears and sambar stags may drink under cover of darkness, while some unknown creature, badger or otter, takes a bath in the cooling stream.

But for leopard-hunting the better parts of the country are low hills intersected by ravines and valleys, the heads of which generally contain water and ample cover of lokandi, jamun, tamarisk, and other green bushes where the great cats find shelter from the burning rays of the sun. There is an abundance of antelope and gazelle; scattered villages afford dogs, goats, calves, and donkeys. Such is the terrain of West Berar to the north of the Nizam's dominions, where a bag of a dozen leopards may be made in a few weeks, as well as nilgai, antelope, gazelle, and many kinds of feathered game.

In such localities leopards may be driven out with a line of beaters, and, standing on the hill-side, one can obtain good sporting shots; the leopard either walks or trots out, sometimes stopping at intervals, or it may cross open ground at a gallop, almost like a flash of light. In such country I have driven out and shot many of these animals, with a force of some 30 or 40 beaters. There was no necessity to tie up goats as bait. We would get all the information of the presence of leopards that was possible, though this was often very meagre, and then start out at daybreak with a definite line of country in view. Experience and a knowledge of the animal's habits enabled us to tell where the beast was likely to be found, and all likely places were examined and the covers beaten systematically.

It was hard work, for it was hot on those stony-hearted hills, even in March, and hotter still in April and May when a burning wind, sometimes laden with dust, blew across the scene. Fortunately the nights were fairly cool. If a leopard was not found in the first beat, we would go on to the next, and so on until the whole line of country had been searched. We were out about twelve hours a day, with a rest of an hour or so at noontide, and an occasional day off. There were many interesting things to observe—gazelle going down to drink in the heat of the day, notwithstanding the views of some naturalists, who probably indulged in a midday siesta, that it is doubtful whether these animals ever drink. Nilgai also drank daily in the middle of the day, and not only every third or fourth day as some have stated. Sandgrouse came down in flocks to their regular drinking-places so punctually that a watch might be set with some accuracy by the arrival of the forerunners, which appeared in small parties between 8.30 and 9 in the morning, and again at 6 in the evening.

Unwounded leopards are not usually dangerous, although I have known one that had been harried in the morning turn on the beaters in the afternoon, and seize by the back of the neck a boy who had come to see the fun. Fortunately the teeth did not penetrate the skull, and the youth recovered. His head was turned to one side, and fixed so for a day or two, but we gradually got it screwed round the right way, and in a few days he was well on the way to recovery. On another occasion a leopard scratched three men who got in its way when it bolted roaring back into the cover from which it had been driven.

But a wounded leopard is a dangerous beast, at any rate in India, though apparently not in Africa, for Mr. A. B. Percival remarks that he has never known one to inflict fatal wounds. In India many sportsmen have been mortally injured in encounters with these beasts, death often supervening from blood-poisoning, sometimes from slight wounds. But it is scarcely correct to say that the leopard is more dangerous than the tiger. It is smaller and so conceals itself more easily, but it seldom kills on the spot, whereas a tiger will usually kill outright, sometimes biting a man almost in half, taking the top off his head, and even using such force that the claws are driven into the body, followed by the toes.

My experience of half a dozen or so men mauled, including myself, is that the victim is not usually worried. The leopard charges with a roar or with continued growls, not springing but *ventre à terre ;* he makes for one's throat, but unconsciously the unarmed person presents his shoulder or puts up an arm to ward off the attack, and is therefore seized by the upper arm and shoulder, claws at the same time being driven into the flesh. There is a short scuffle, and in a moment the attacking beast, after inflicting a bite or two, retreats to cover. Its foul breath in the face is unpleasant.

But sometimes a leopard does stay to worry its victim. Mr. Gilbert, a well-known Bombay sportsman, shot one which had seized one of his men, making a large hole in his chest with its claws, penetrating to the lungs. The man was bitten and clawed all over, and died in a few hours, but the chest wound was the worst. The leopard did not leave him until it was shot some three minutes after the seizure, and when Gilbert arrived on the scene it was worrying and shaking him as a dog does a rat. Three officers whom I recollect being mauled, one having only a claw-wound in the wrist, died of blood-poisoning within a week. Natives generally recover, but a shikari who was with me when I shot the man-eating tiger was killed next year by a leopard. A Brinjara who used to accompany me in Berar was afterwards killed by a leopard. He was hunting one with dog and spear, but it evaded his spear-thrust and bit and clawed him badly. He lived about a week.

A leopard will run up a tree like a cat, and people have not infrequently been pulled down and killed. Baldwin[1] relates that in the neighbourhood of Kampti an officer of the artillery and a native shikari were both pulled out of a tree and mortally wounded. The officer fired at and wounded the brute as it passed below the bough on which he was sitting. It climbed up, pulled him

[1] *The Large and Small Game of Bengal.* By Captain J. H. Baldwin. Kegan Paul. 1877.

down, mauled him, and then climbed up again and killed the native. Many similar instances showing that there is no safety in a tree could be called to mind. I remember one sportsman, always very careful of himself, who used to have a zariba of thorn bushes constructed round the base of the tree in which he sat to await the arrival of a leopard. In following up wounded leopards a gun loaded with buckshot cartridges is most effective. It is not easy to shoot with a bullet a charging animal which presents a small mark.

A wounded leopard is a gallant beast and will fight to the last, as in an incident related in the long-defunct *Oriental Sporting Magazine*, where one of these animals, having killed a bullock, was tracked by a party of native hunters into a garden. The men advanced cautiously with loaded matchlocks, when the leopard charged, and was slightly wounded by a man who fired and was instantly pulled down and killed ; it struck down three more before they could raise their guns. It then crouched in a small bush, and lay growling until they again advanced to within ten yards, blowing their matches, but out of six matchlocks only two exploded, and the leopard dashed among them and pulled another man down. Men armed with swords and spears then rushed in and hewed the beast to pieces. Seven men were carried from the ground on conclusion of the conflict, and of these two never spoke again.

Indian villagers often show remarkable courage in dealing with wild beasts. It is recorded in the Bombay Natural History Society's Journal that on the 12th March, 1896, in a village a few miles from Dwarka, in Kathiawar, a leopard was seen to take shelter in a small stack on an open plain. A number of Wagher tribesmen turned out with sticks and surrounded the stack; after a time the beast broke cover and flew at a Wagher, whom he seized by the throat and brought to the ground. The other men at once attacked the leopard, forcing it to release its hold before any serious damage was done. It then went for another man, who pluckily stood his ground and closed with it by seizing it round the body, the two falling to the ground together. The leopard then made tracks for the village; a running fight was kept up for about a hundred yards and the brute was unable to evade the blows of the pursuers. One of these hung on to its tail, thus retarding its progress, while another, armed with an axe, rushed upon it and dealt it a death-blow, splitting the skull. It is satisfactory to know that all the wounded recovered.

But the people are sometimes extraordinarily cowardly or apathetic. In May 1895, not far from my camp, it was reported that a child had been carried off by a leopard. The poor boy might have been saved, but when he called for help the people shut themselves up in their houses instead of attempting to rescue him.

In Hyderabad a trapped leopard was sometimes let loose for spearing on the open plain. The "sport" was generally poor, for the beast would crouch as one rider after another galloped past and thrust his spear in if he could get his horse near enough. It was while thus spearing a leopard on Bolarum Plain that a famous sportsman, Colonel Nightingale, died on horseback in 1868 from the bursting of a blood-vessel on the brain. Leopards have often been put up and speared by pig-stickers.

CHAPTER XIII

THE LEOPARD OF NANDA

LEOPARDS are among the most terrible of man-eaters. In March 1899 I was shooting tigers in a valley below the deserted fort of Manikgarh, near the northern border of Hyderabad State, one of those massive mountain strongholds which, witnesses to the turbulent times of a more heroic age, stand on many lofty hill-tops of Southern India. However, I am not here concerned with the tigers that were killed during this expedition. They were, except for their cattle-killing propensities, harmless creatures not given to molesting man. Far otherwise was a man-eating leopard, of which Mr. Inverarity told the history,[1] involving poignant and dramatic human tragedies when he was encamped in the same place five years before. This murderous brute infested a group of villages scattered over an area some seven miles in diameter. A number of people had already been carried off when Inverarity pitched his camp on the 25th April, 1894. He had not long to wait for a kill.

On the night of April 26th a man was killed at a small hamlet two miles from the camp. He saw the corpse, that of a fine strong man, who had been seized

[1] This account is taken from the *Journal of the Bombay Natural History Society*.

by the throat as he was lying asleep on his cot in front of his hut, his wife on another cot beside him. The leopard's tracks showed that it had crossed the fields, entered the village, and passed through a gate that had not been closed. The beast was driven off by the shouts of the villagers, and retreated by the same way into the jungle, which was flat, intersected by shallow nullahs, and in some places having patches of tall grass. In such country, extending for miles, it was practically impossible to track down or beat out the animal.

On the night of April 28th another man was killed in a neighbouring village, Chandur, where my own was pitched in 1899, and where the deeds of this man-eater were still fresh in the minds of the inhabitants. The leopard was frightened off, and afterwards visited Inverarity's camp, and came close to the tents; it then carried off a dog. Two days later a boy of seven, the son of the dealer who supplied the camp, was killed at Nanda, four miles from Chandur. The boy was sleeping on the same cot as a man in the open space in front of an outside hut of the village, the boy being furthest from the road. The leopard passed the man, seized the boy, carried him away, and devoured him in the jungle. Not a vestige of the body was found.

On the night of May 6th a woman was killed at Nimni, 7 miles off, and the camp was moved to Nanda, where the next kill was expected. On the night of May 9th Inverarity heard an uproar at a house in the village 80 yards off. He was on the spot in two minutes, with lamp and rifle, and saw the track where the body had been dragged down the village road. Followed by a number of villagers, all shouting at the top of their voices, he ran along the trail, and in 50 yards came to a large patch of blood where the leopard had evidently dropped the body; he had taken it up again; a few yards farther on the road cleared the houses and took a sharp turn to the left into a field, and, soon after rounding the corner, the pursuers ran on to the body. The leopard had just left, as there was no blood when they first arrived and in a few minutes a large pool formed. At first it looked like the body of a grey-haired woman, but it turned out to be a girl of about sixteen years; the hair being full of dust looked grey in the lamp-light. She was dead; the body lay on the back, the legs straight out, the head resting on the right cheek, the right arm, adorned with two iron bangles, was bent as if it had been thrown up towards the neck, the left arm lay along the side. There was a cut an inch long on the chin, and the fatal teeth-marks in the throat. As they looked the blood poured out from a hole in the neck just behind the lobe of the right ear, forming a large pool of black blood on the ground; the jugular vein had been opened. If they had gone quietly there would have been a good chance of a shot, for the leopard was evidently very reluctant to leave its victim. But of course the shouting cannot be prevented, as the man-eater might be frightened away by the noise before the victim was dead, though in this case death must have been immediate. The expression of the face was quite calm.

The leopard was tracked some distance down the road and across the fields, where there were patches of cover, while the jungle was half a mile off. He had gone at a walk. The relatives would not leave the body where it lay, so that the beast might be shot when it returned. They insisted on sitting round it with a number of sympathising friends, making a great noise. The tracks were those of a large male leopard. The girl must have weighed seven stone. When the teeth are in the wounds, no blood flows, so none was found on the trail except the large patch where the body was dropped.

The girl had been lying with seven other people all close together on the ground in the open space in front of the hut. She was nearest the road. The leopard entered by a gap between the corner of the hut and the thorn fence, and then had the girl's throat within reach. She was buried in the morning, and in the evening Inverarity sat close to the place where she was found for five hours till the moon set, staring at the road in case the man-eater should come up it. But it did not return. Nothing further happened until May 15th, when a large male leopard was caught in a pitfall at the entrance to the village of Nanda, close to the spot where it had dropped the girl on the 9th. The bait was a goat, and the brute was shot in the trap by a policeman.

The man-eater was supposed to be done with, but that very night in the same village a leopard seized a sleeping police-constable. He was lying on his right side with his left arm over his head, so the leopard did not get a good grip at his neck; it was frightened off. The man walked to the camp, and was there by daylight. He had a shallow wound on the jaw, another not more than half an inch deep in the back of the arm, and a slight scratch on the back. The wounds were probed and washed out with a solution of carbolic acid. He kept well that day, but next morning his cheek and neck were much swollen; at night he breathed with difficulty and he died at midnight, 44 hours after being wounded, no doubt from blood-poisoning.

This leopard was thought to be a female, judging from the size of the holes in the victim's neck. There had not been more than one track at the scene of a kill, but as the two animals were at the same place the same night, they were probably a pair. Between April 26th and May 9th there were five kills, making in all 26 deaths before the policeman was seized. All the others were killed at once, but only in the case of the boy did the leopard get away with the body. There were no more kills, and probably the male had done all the killing. The dead leopard had a perfect set of teeth and skin in good order, and there appeared no reason for its taking to man-eating. All the kills were at night, of persons asleep, and there was no instance of anyone up and about being attacked either by day or night.

In the case of a man-eating leopard in the Sundarbans, where tigers are, or were perhaps the commoner animal of the two, a respectable Bengali babu was carried off. The narrator was, he says, just falling asleep, when his shikari told him that an animal was carrying off a deer he had shot. He mustered all hands, including the brother of the dead babu, and followed the animal, a leopard, into a patch of thick jungle, where it sat panting. It then moved across a ravine into another patch, and on tracking it down they saw a cub and another leopard feasting on a human body. Shots were fired, and when the smoke cleared they saw the beast "making awful grimaces and on the eve of charging." One of the shikaris fired and the brute made a leap at him, but another shot finished it off. They then examined the body on which the leopards were making a meal. The state of decomposition of the corpse, and the horrible condition in which it lay, without arms or legs, prevented a near approach; but from the cloth and some silver charms tied about the waist it was identified as that of the babu's late brother.

Leopards have always been destructive in the Central Provinces. One infested a tract of country about 40 miles south of Nagpur for more than two years, and was known to have killed more than a hundred women and children. The villages were generally situated close to watercourses fringed with jungle, which sometimes extended close up to the houses, affording good cover for beasts of prey. This leopard went a round of eight or ten villages, never remaining two days together in one patch of jungle. "The village children would be at play in the village gardens, or a group of girls and women would be drawing water from the well sunk in the watercourse, when in the twinkling of an eye the spotted fiend would be in their midst, holding on with bloodthirsty grip to the throat of a helpless victim. A burst of screams and a frantic rush of women and children would instantly follow; but by the time the men who happened to be at home could catch up clubs and spears and sally out, nothing but a little spilt blood would remain to reveal the tragedy which had just taken place." The beast began to enter villages boldly at nightfall, and even invaded the courtyards of houses and carried off children from the very doorsteps. It was at last shot by a police-constable.

Another leopard used to lie in wait for people near the village of Nachingaon on the Wurdah river, and was also in the habit of pulling down watchmen from their platforms raised on poles in the middle of the fields, where they sat to scare deer and hog from the crops at night. The man-eater would swarm up the poles and pull the watchman from his perch when he slept during the night. One victim was an idiot who was sleeping out in the open air as usual when the village was awakened by a frightful yell. The idiot had been seized and so mangled that he died as they lifted him from the ground. This leopard was caught and shot in a box-trap.

Captain Forsyth shot one in a cow-house, where it had killed a number of cattle. This animal used to take up a position in the high crops surrounding a village, and would kill women and children who ventured outside the village precincts. It had been wounded by a shikari with a bullet through the external ear and one paw, and thus rendered incapable of killing game. Sterndale tells of a leopard—he calls it a " pard "—which killed over three hundred people during its reign of terror in the Seoni district of the Central Provinces. It seemed to kill for killing's sake, and often the victims, sometimes three in one night, were untouched except for the fatal wound in the throat.

As is always the case when a man-eater is about, the countryside was demoralized; animals ravaged the fields and the people feared to go to their work. Sterndale was out in camp after this monster, and was told piteous tales of its deeds; some who were so fortunate as to escape from the beast's clutches showed their scars; two children told their stories; one had witnessed the death of a sister, the other of a brother, for the leopard went boldly to work in broad daylight. The beast was regarded as a transformed human being, for it was the one of which the story of the change from human form to that of a leopard was related by Forsyth. When Sterndale was out at night watching for this animal, he heard the villagers calling out from house to house hourly—"Are you awake, brothers? Are you awake?" He scoured the country by day, and at night his camp was surrounded by great fires, his people were made to sleep inside tents, and the doors were guarded by sentries with musket and bayonet. But the fires would of themselves have been of no use, for man-eaters do not fear fires, but only the watchers to whom they may be betrayed by the glow of burning wood. On one occasion a woman was found bitterly crying in a field; beside her lay the dead body of her husband. He had been seized by the throat and dragged across the fire made at the entrance of the little hut in which they had spent the night watching their crops. The woman hung on to her husband's legs and exerted her strength against the man-eater's, shrieking aloud. It dropped the body and fled, making no attempt to molest her or her little child. Two other men were killed that night. This fiend was at last shot in the dusk by a native shikari.

Not only the Central Provinces in general, but the Seoni District in particular has always had a bad reputation for man-eaters. In 1901 a leopard killed 20 people in rapid succession within 15 miles of Gunsore village. On April 10th Mr. W. A. Conduitt heard of a kill, and found the body of the victim in a mangled condition with one arm torn right off, lying in a nullah within 200 yards of a village. The animal had come at midnight, and had killed and dragged away the body from just outside a hut where four people were sleeping, but none of them heard the slightest sound. The leopard came back that night, but it was so dark that it was inadvisable to shoot, although it could be dis tinctly heard at the body. On April 21st there was a kill at another village where the beast entered a house and dragged the body away into an open plain 30 yard off. There were two children asleep in the house at the time, but they were not disturbed. Only the chest head, and neck were mauled, and a good deal of fles eaten off those parts. Conduitt hung a hurricane lam on a pole 5 feet high and 20 feet from the body covering one side of the lamp with a cloth so as the afford a dark line of approach for man-eater. The beast came to the corpse of its victim before midnigh and was at once shot dead.

There are seldom man-eating tigers in Hyderabad Deccan, although leopards are not uncommon. In February 1891, Mr. Davies, Deputy Commissioner of Basim, in Berar, shot a leopard which had just begun to prey on human beings. A party of travellers were on their way to the Nizam's dominions, and had put up for the night in a spot surrounded by wooded hills Shortly after midnight a woman who was one of the party was disturbed by feeling the covering of her 12 year-old boy roughly dragged away, and at once missed her son. She raised the alarm, but in the darkness of the night with no lights search was impossible, and the poor mother had to wait in terror for what the morning might bring. When dawn came her fear were confirmed. Spots of blood and the track of the body dragged through the grass revealed the nature the tragedy. The people followed, and in a of watercourse close by the skull was found stripped flesh and hair. They pursued the trail up a dark ravine, and at the foot of a mohwa tree they came upon the coarse cloth with which the mother had covered her son's neck, soaked with blood. Looking up the tree the horrified searchers saw the headless trunk of the unfortunate boy balanced across a large bough, the legs crossed and one arm stiffly extended.

Mr. Davies was fortunately in camp five miles off, and to him they appealed, as natives always confidently appeal to a white man. He went to the place and had a hole dug in the ground near the mohwa tree, and in it concealed himself in the afternoon with a covering of thorns, in the hope that the man-eater would return to the body of its victim before dark. But the night became so black that nothing could be seen, and he returned to camp, first making efforts to get the men to bring away the body so that it should not be further fed upon. But no money nor threats would persuade them to touch it. They were sure that the spirit of the dead had already turned into an animal which, acting in sympathy with the leopard, had warned the brute of danger. Thorns were therefore placed all round the tree in the hope of keeping the beast off. Vain hope! In the morning the thorns were found pushed aside. The cloth and the corpse had both been removed.

Tracks led up the ravine in which the leopard had evidently taken up its abode, and at once preparations were made to beat it out. Men were collected, and with drums beating they entered one side of the cover, Mr. Davies posting himself at the other. But an opening was left by the cowardice of some of the men, and the monster crossed a glade at speed and disappeared into another ravine. Out of this it was driven, but gave a wide berth to the gun. Three times it escaped, but was at last driven into a small ravine and hemmed in completely. The beaters advanced once more, throwing stones until they had actually reached the bottom, when the beast sprang up at their very feet and crossed 150 yards off, a long and uncertain shot as it was going fast. However, the bullet sped true, striking it in the neck and turning it over dead on the spot.

A shout of joy burst from all, and with acclamation the dead brute was carried to the village where the camp was pitched, the people shouting repeatedly—"Victory to Davies Sahib!" As they passed through the village, the women turned out, each with a brass dish furnished with a small lighted wick, red powder, and two small copper coins. A post-mortem led to the finding of three fingers of the victim who had thus tragically met his death. It is probable that this leopard would have become a confirmed man-eater, for it had already killed two people, and severely hurt a third. The dogs in the villages within a four-mile radius had nearly all been carried off, and as the supply diminished, a baby was snatched through the open door of a hut; and an attack was made on an elderly woman, who recovered. The leopard, a female with a good coat, was in milk, but the cubs could not be found. No doubt she had taken to killing human beings in order to supply her offspring with tender meat.

Only three months after this tragedy I had occasion to deal with a leopard that had taken to man-eating near Ellichpur, in another part of the Province of Berar. I rode out to the place on a scorching day in May. The beast was in the habit of going a round of several villages in search of stray dogs and goats, and had picked up a child or two. At the village where I decided to stay for the night a little girl had been carried off the night before; nothing remained but a tiny hand with yellow palm, a tress of hair, a rag, and a string of beads. The river, now nearly dry, ran through a cultivated tract, and had extensive patches of bush upon the banks, which were intersected by innumerable fissures. In this maze of jungle and ravine it was useless to search. At night my bed was placed in the shadow of a hut, with two goats picketed not far from the head. It was a dark night, but there was a view of the sky-line on the edge of the rising ground on which the hamlet was built. I slept with my rifle beside me.

At about three o'clock in the morning I awoke; the goats coughed hoarsely and pulled at their tethers; and as I looked, the dark form of a leopard was for a moment defined against the sky-line. The animal, coming towards me, was swallowed up in the gloom; I reached down for my rifle, and it must have seen the movement, for the next instant it appeared again on the sky-line, making off. A shot elicited a growl, and the beast disappeared. Men ran out with lanterns; we followed in the direction taken by the leopard, but could see nothing. The morning showed no sign on the hard ground, either of tracks or blood. But the depredations ceased from that time; and a few days later a leopard with a broken leg was killed by the villagers some miles away.

This brute had not only taken children, but had begun to attack people in the fields by day; report said that it was a man turned into a wild beast on having a stone thrown at him by his wife; those who had been attacked and wounded declared that it was black and tailless. In fact, the usual myths had gathered round the creature. It may be remarked that no glaring eyes were to be seen in the dark, as is commonly supposed to be the case with the great cats, or all cats. I recollect, when in camp on one occasion, two glowing orbs were visible from my tent, and were thought by an Indian officer who was with me to be the eyes of a leopard. We walked towards them, and when we arrived at the spot found a pair of glow-worms with the distance between them that would be expected in a leopard's eyes. The eyes do not of themselves shine in the dark, but they reflect a light without the presence of which they cannot be seen.

Near one of my camps a leopard stepped over a sleeping dog and carried off and devoured a child which was lying beside its father. At another place one entered a hut, tried to drag a woman away, and on being driven off rushed into another hut and carried off and ate a boy who was seized by the throat and uttered no sound. The forest was so dense and extensive that it was useless to attempt to drive the beast out, and a night-long vigil over a goat was spent in vain.

In 1902 Mr. L. S. Osmaston killed in the Nasik District a leopard which had taken to man-eating in the Mulher Valley. There had been a severe famine during which many people died in the jungle in the adjoining native state, the first victim of the leopard being probably one dying or asleep in the forest. It killed in all some thirty people and wounded eleven others. When the beast first took to man-eating it would take no one unless it was quite dark and the person lying down. It would enter a hut and lay hold of one of the sleepers. If the victim was seized by the throat he could not cry out, and he was carried off before the other sleepers knew anything. If an arm or leg was seized, the outcry sent him off. But he became bolder, and his last victims but one were a woman and her child who were killed in broad daylight; the bodies were not found.

Osmaston made many attempts to kill this brute, but was not successful until November 1902, when he heard of a boy of fifteen being killed. This unfortunate lad had been seized by the leg a year before, but, tended by Mr. and Mrs. Osmaston, had made a good recovery. This time he and a few others were sitting close to a bright fire on a threshing-floor near the village in the early part of the night when the beast carried him off a quarter of a mile, and ate most of the head, the flesh of one leg, and all the inside. There were no trees near the kill, so a cart was taken off its wheels and placed on four posts about eight feet high, driven into the ground, and covered with brushwood, a hole being made to shoot through. In this ambush Osmaston took up his position 35 feet from the corpse in the afternoon, and at 5.30 he heard the leopard growl close behind him, it could not have seen him, so he thought it must have scented him. When it was dark, he turned up his hurricane lamp and hung it on a post so that the light shone on the body.

At 8.30 he saw the leopard beyond the kill. When it got to the body he fired both barrels at once as the lamp always went out with the concussion, and no second shot could be obtained. After the flash and report he heard the beast crashing down the hill for some five seconds, then quiet, then a groaning growl.

He returned to the village, and at daybreak followed the tracks of blood, found the beast still alive, and finished it off with a shot in the head. It was a fine male. The shots fired in the night had struck it in the stomach and broken a hind-leg. This is an interesting instance, showing the leopard's development as a man-eater, its indifference to fire, and the possible exercise of the sense of scent.

The leopard does not appear to be so dangerous or persistent a man-eater in Africa as it is in India. Vaughan Kirby never heard of a man-eater of this species. Roosevelt heard of one at Neri, which had killed seven children in the daytime, the victims being little boys who were watching the flocks of goats; sometimes it took a boy, sometimes a goat. It was killed by two old men with spears when it took its last victim, and was a big male, very old and emaciated, with teeth worn down to stumps. At Meru a leopard had seized a woman by the throat and eaten her; another was attacked but escaped. This was also old with worn teeth. In another case a Masai chief was seized with claws only by the head and hand when he was sitting under a bush to eat with a few followers. Sir Alfred Pease mentions a leopard taking women and children, and Kittenberger says that at night leopards in Africa will enter dwellings and often kill human beings, and that they turn man-eaters more frequently than do lions. He tells of a dog taken out of a tent although fires were blazing all round. In fact, the idea that fires are of themselves a deterrent has been proved to be fallacious in the case of all carnivores. In another instance in Africa a leopard broke into a hut, attacked a sick woman, and took to flight when the villagers turned out. But while they were after it, the animal returned and again attacked the woman. A man passing heard her moaning, entered the hut, met the leopard face to face and clubbed it to death.

In the Congo between Ruchuru and Stanleyville leopards took to lying in wait for mail-runners whose remains were often found among the scattered letters.

CHAPTER XIV

JAGUARS, PUMAS, AND HYENAS

LITERATURE dealing with the great cats of America, the pumas and jaguars, is rather scanty. The jaguar bears much resemblance to the leopard both in size, structure, and coloration. The black rosettes are larger than those of the leopard, and they contain a central spot; such a spot, less profusely distributed, has, however, been observed in some Indian leopards; I shot one in Berar having this characteristic marking. The jaguar is found from Texas in the north to the northern limits of Patagonia in the south. Its habits are largely arboreal, especially in the great river systems of the Orinoco and the Amazons, where flood and marsh drive many mammals to take to the trees. As in the case of the leopard, black jaguars are not uncommon, the spots showing in the light.

A brief account of the animal is given in Darwin's *Voyage of the Beagle;* and there is further information in Hudson's *Naturalist in La Plata.* Its favourite haunts are the wooded banks of the great rivers, but south of the Plata they frequented the reeds bordering lakes, an interesting instance of adaptation to environment comparable with that of the tiger, which still occupies the reed-beds of northern Asia, from whence it is supposed to have migrated into the forests of

India and Malaya. The jaguar resembles the tiger in requiring the proximity of water. Its chief prey is the capybara, and where this animal is plentiful there is little for man to fear from the jaguar.

Jaguars, called "tigers," were, however, given to man-killing on the Parana, where, Darwin says, they had killed many wood-cutters and even entered vessels at night. A man who came up on deck was seized by a jaguar, but escaped with the loss of an arm. They were said to be most dangerous when driven from the islands of the Parana by floods. Darwin was told that a few years before his visit in 1831 a very large one found its way into a church at Sante Fé, and two priests who entered were killed, one after another, while a third, who went to see what had happened to the other two, escaped with difficulty. It is not recorded whether there was any attempt at eating the bodies. The beast was shot from an unroofed corner of the church.

The gauchos say that the jaguar is followed by yelping foxes at night, as the tiger is attended by jackals. It is a noisy animal, roaring much, especially before bad weather. This roaring habit is confirmed by Waterton, who heard one but was told it was a puma. However, his people went to the place in a canoe, and saw an immense jaguar standing on the trunk of an aged tree which bent over the river; it growled and showed its teeth when they approached, but made off when fired at. On another occasion he was awakened at midnight by an Indian who called his attention to the approach of a jaguar, and he heard the softly sounding tread of its feet. The moon had gone down, but every now and then he could get a glance at the animal by the light of the fire. Whenever the fire got low, the jaguar came a little nearer, and when the Indian renewed it, he retired abruptly. Sometimes he came within twenty yards, when they had a view of him sitting up on his hind-legs like a dog, and they could at times hear him pacing to and fro. At last the Indian gave a yell, and the jaguar made off. It appears that the animal was not afraid of the fire itself, but of the human beings who were observing it in the light; and it is easy to understand that, with the preconceived notions of the ferocity of carnivorous animals prevalent in those times, the naturalist might ascribe his supposed safety from attack to the existence of the fire rather than to the vigilance of the watchers, or to the probability that the animal had no aggressive intentions.

Bates also heard the roar of jaguars in the jungle about a furlong distant, and, having read in books of travel of tigers coming to warm themselves by the fires of a bivouac, "thought this strong wish to witness the same sight would have been gratified." It is to be feared that books of travel have to answer for many false ideas; the jaguars approached within twenty yards, as evident from tracks seen in the morning. Bates found on the Amazons the mangled remains of an alligator that had been killed by a jaguar which had eaten all except the head and forequarters and the hard inedible parts.

Hartwig, in *The Tropical World*, describes the jaguar as "the most formidable of the tyrants of the North American solitudes except the grizzly and the polar bears"; these animals are not tyrants, and the bears are not formidable or aggressive, nor is the jaguar generally a confirmed man-eater. The same writer gives some absurd descriptions of the hunting of the jaguar, but most of these old writers appear to have regarded wild beasts as always ready to attack man at sight; he says that the jaguar, "far from being afraid of man, springs upon him when alone." He relates, however, a probable story that in northern Peru a jaguar took a ten-year-old boy out of his hammock in the hut of an English settler, and devoured him; this animal, like the leopard, will very likely take a child when opportunity offers.

Hudson, *The Naturalist in La Plata*, gives an account of jaguar-hunting by a gaucho, who was famous for his boldness and dexterity on the Pampas, where these animals were numerous. The jaguar was surrounded when it was crouching among some clumps of tall pampas grass, when the hunter uncoiled his lasso and proceeded in a leisurely manner to form the loop. But he had, like some others of us, become careless and made the mistake of allowing his restive horse to turn aside from the hunted animal. The jaguar burst from the cover, sprang on the haunches of the horse, and dragged the hunter down by his cloak; it would have killed him, but another man lassoed it round the neck, and it was pulled off and killed. The man was not hurt, but rode off home alone, disgusted with his failure. On the way back this same hunter saw a puma which sat up looking at him. He dismounted and struck at it with his hunting-knife; but the animal evaded the blow and dealt him a stroke with its paw, clawing his cheek down so that the bone was exposed. The puma then trotted away. The man had his wound dressed, but was marked for life; his temper changed, and he became morose and sensitive, never joining again in hunting expeditions.

The puma has a reputation for gentleness and even benevolence towards human beings, so it is not surprising that we have in the story of Maldonada a counterpart of that of Androcles and the lion, and perhaps with more grounds for authenticity, for it is related by Rui Diaz in his history of La Plata. Maldonada, condemned to death, was tied to a forest tree so that the wild beasts might destroy her; but two days afterwards she was discovered unharmed, having been protected, she said, by a puma, which remained at her side and drove off all wild animals that attempted to molest her. There seems, however, no particular reason why they should molest her! Hudson relates the story of an injured man lying on the Pampas, when a puma came and sat near him, and afterwards attacked and drove off a jaguar which appeared on the scene during the night.

There are many such stories, some of which bear too close a likeness to one another. The origin of this friendliness to man which, says Hudson, is well known, is mysterious; he suggests that possibly the human form or countenance or odour may inspire it. Gay, in his *Natural History of Chili*, says: "When attacked by man its energy and daring at once forsake it, and it becomes a weak, inoffensive animal, and trembling, and uttering piteous moans, and shedding abundant tears, it seems to implore compassion from a generous enemy." Yet this animal, so timid in the presence of man, will always attack the jaguar, and apparently with success; while in North America it is said to be similarly hostile to the grizzly bear.

C. B. Brown gives an account of a meeting with a puma which shows that, like so many people in regard to carnivorous animals, he started with the assumption of the ferocity of this comparatively harmless and inoffensive creature. Nor did his experience induce him to change his views, for in his description of the " noble but appalling sight " of the animal crouching in front of him and remaining motionless 15 yards off, he says that he waved his arms and shouted, and the puma then turned and bounded off; it would have been surprising if it had not done so, for it must have been as alarmed as Brown himself, who considered that he had had a narrow escape from being killed and eaten!

In view of the character of the puma as portrayed in South America, it may be asked why it is included among the potential man-eaters. There is certainly little evidence against the animal. Darwin relates that two men and a woman were killed in Chili, but they may have been protecting their cattle, and he does not say that they were eaten. In North America, however, it has been given a different character, although not generally supposed to be inimical to man. It is related on the authority of a Mr. Perry that in the spring of 1886 three children were returning from school at Olympia, Washington, when the eldest boy of twelve saw what he thought was a large yellow dog trotting behind them. The youngest boy of six was behind the others when he was suddenly rolled over in front of them, and a puma sprang over their heads, seized the small child in its mouth, and vanished in the bushes. The elder brother, with only a bottle in his hand, went in and rescued the child, beating the puma over the head with the bottle, and then attempting to gouge out its eyes with the jagged edges of the broken neck. This certainly looks like a case of attempted man-eating. It is interesting to note that this animal, like the tiger and leopard, will cover up a carcass when it has eaten its fill, to protect it from the vultures and so preserve it for another meal.

In British Columbia a Swedish sailor was wielding his spade to clear a space in the forest when a puma seized him by the arm, and it was only after a long struggle, in which he was severely injured, that he succeeded in killing it with his spade. Probably the puma had no man-eating intentions, but its young may have been concealed close by. A few years ago a circumstantial account appeared in the press of an attack by a puma in British Columbia on two children, one of whom beat the animal off.

The gauchos of the Pampas hunt the puma with dogs, against which the beast defends itself to the last, while taking no notice of the men with them and not even retaliating when struck. Darwin was told that at Tandeel, south of La Plata, within three months 100 pumas were entangled with the bolas, then lassoed, and dragged along the ground until insensible. In Chili they are driven into trees and then shot or baited with dogs. The lasso is made of very strong, well-plaited raw hide. One end is attached to the surcingle of the saddle, the other terminates in a small metal ring, by which a noose can be formed. When in use the gaucho keeps a small coil in his bridle-hand, holding in the other the running noose about eight feet in diameter. He whirls this round his head, keeping the noose open by the dexterous movement of his wrist; then, throwing it, he causes it to fall on the chosen spot.

The bolas consists of three round stones covered with leather, or of wooden or iron balls, united by a thin plaited thong about eight feet long. The gaucho holds the smallest of the three in his hand and whirls the other two round and round his head ; then, taking aim, sends them like a chain shot revolving through the air. When they strike the object they wind round it, crossing each other and become firmly hitched. By a man riding at speed they can be whirled with effect at a distance of eighty yards.

Commodore Byron, in his *Narrative of the Loss of the Wager*, describes an experience with a puma in Tierra del Fuego. Some of his men saw a large beast in a wood, and after they had lain down to rest by a fire, one of the men was disturbed by an animal blowing in his face. He had the presence of mind to snatch a brand and thrust it at the nose of the beast, which made off. It was evidently not afraid of fire.

Darwin relates that when at supper at the Rio Tapalguen he was suddenly struck with horror thinking that he was eating one of the favourite dishes of the country, a half-formed calf long before its proper time of birth. It turned out to be puma ; the meat was very white, and remarkably like veal in taste. Dr. Shaw was laughed at for saying that the flesh of the lion was held in great esteem, having no small affinity with veal both in colour, taste, and flavour. The gauchos differ in their opinion as to whether the jaguar is good eating, but are unanimous in saying that cat is excellent. Having presided at the skinning of some dozens of tigers and leopards in India, I would certainly not wish to taste animals so offensive to the nostrils !

Hyenas are generally regarded as cowardly and

disgusting animals. They live principally on carrion, and their taste for human corpses makes them especially repulsive. They possess great strength of teeth and jaws, enabling them to crack the largest bones. They cannot be called "game," and usually they are not shot, but they afford a good run with horse and spear. The hyena will not retaliate even when wounded, although the panther appears to be afraid of it, and will give way to it at a kill. In a fight recorded in the *Journal of the Bombay Natural History Society*, a hyena got the better of a panther.

The striped hyena, found in Asia and Africa, and the African spotted hyena have both been known to attack man. Baldwin says that hyenas sometimes enter a hut and carry off a sleeping child. The mortality bill for one year shows 33 human beings killed by hyenas; probably most of these were children. General E. F. Burton relates that a woman was fetching water from a stream near her village in the Shevaroy Hills in South India, when a hyena rushed from the jungle, seized her by the arm, and tried to drag her away. She dropped her water-vessel, but the hyena would not let go, and she in turn seized the beast by the ears and attempted to drag it towards the village. The villagers, attracted by her cries, rushed up and found her on the ground struggling with the hyena. They attacked it with clubs, but it would not let go until they had slashed it about the head with knives. Then it released one arm only to grip the other; but it was at last killed. It was a female, and probably had cubs near by. The woman died. There is in Palestine a superstition akin to that regarding the wolf in other countries. A spell may be cast over the traveller, obliging him to follow the unclean beast to its lair, when the human being can be released from the spell only by shedding his own blood. It is related that a schoolboy was returning from Jerusalem to his home on the Mount of Olives when he met a hyena. He managed to resist the spell, but on his recounting the adventure at home, his father at once caused him to be bled, and so saved him from all possible evil consequences.

White children are guarded with the greatest care in far countries, not only by the parents but by faithful native servants whose devotion to their charges has always been remarkable and was an outstanding feature in the troublous times of the Indian Mutiny. It is almost unheard of, therefore, for a white infant to be carried off by a wild animal, and but one instance is recorded. An officer and his family were living in tents on the race-course at Bellary, when on a moonlight night the ayah in charge of a baby in a small tent left her charge for a short time. On her return she saw a hyena coming out of the tent with a white bundle in its mouth. She raised a yell which brought out the mother, who gave chase and the beast dropped the bundle; it contained the baby, fortunately well wrapped up and uninjured.

The spotted hyena of Africa is stronger and larger than the striped one. It is bold in its depredations. Bruce relates that one entered his tent and stood near the head of his bed, munching some bundles of candles. Bruce struck it with a pike, and it dropped the candles and tried to run up the shaft to get at its assailant, who was obliged to shoot the hyena with a pistol while at the same time his servant cleft its skull with a battle-axe. Sir Samuel Baker was roused at night by his wife when a hyena entered the tent; he shot it as he was afraid it would eat his saddles. Sir Alfred Pease[1] was also roused by his wife in similar circumstances, but did not get a shot. He knew a hyena to carry a saddle out of an occupied tent and eat all but the stirrup-irons. On another occasion a friend of his sleeping on the ground awoke to find an animal "breathing an awful breath and glaring in his face"; he thought it was a lion, but he could only describe it as "too terrible and hideous for words"; it was more probably a hyena.

In the Deccan I have shot a striped hyena in a beat with a charge of small shot; though only wounded, it made no attempt to retaliate when I went close up to finish it off. An officer at Ellichpur woke up to see one standing by his bed; it had probably come after his dog, for which these animals have a special predilection.

The spotted hyena is a confirmed man-eater when his victims are the weak and helpless. Sir Harry Johnston sent a sick man back a short distance to the coast by himself. In the night he was attacked and severely bitten by hyenas; he beat them off and recovered from his wounds. They will take children from huts, and attack and devour wounded men.[2] Roosevelt says they will carry away even sleeping adults, and they will prey on people weakened by famine and disease. In 1908–9 spotted hyenas burst though the hedges made round the camps formed for sleeping-sickness patients and carried off and ate the dying, so that armed sentries had to be posted round the camp at night. One of Pease's native hunters was seized by a hyena as he slept beside the camp-fire and part of his face was torn off. So fire

[1] *The Book of the Lion.* By Sir Alfred Pease. John Murray.
[2] *African Game Trails.* By Theodore Roosevelt. John Murray.

affords no safety from hyenas any more than from other man-eaters. Major Coryndon, when sleeping beside his wagon in North-West Rhodesia, was seized by the hand and dragged out of bed by a hyena. His hand was badly lacerated, but he returned to bed with his rifle beside him, and when the beast came back, shot it dead. That hyenas are not kept off by fire was further proved by a traveller in Abyssinia, who had large fires and a guard posted, but in the night ravening hyenas burst into the camp and stampeded the ponies and mules.

CHAPTER XV

WOLVES

THERE are many species of wolves, wild dogs and jackals, all of which, belonging to the dog tribe, may claim affinity. The European wolf (*Canis lupus*), at one time infesting the British Isles, still inhabits a great part of Europe in suitable localities, extending also through Asia, and across the Behring Straits into North America. In Asia there are local races, which differ from the European wolf only as much as would be expected from the nature of their environment. Thus the Indian wolf is classed as a separate species by naturalists, although to the unscientific observer the sole difference between it and the European wolf is its smaller size and lighter build, features which would be expected in an animal found in a hot country as in the plains of Hindustan. The *chanko* or black wolf of Tibet is termed a separate species mainly because it possesses under-fur, which has, no doubt, been developed owing to climatic conditions, and without which the animal would probably be unable to survive the icy winds of the lofty uplands in high Asia.

Wolves survived in parts of the British Isles up to some two hundred years ago. In the time of Edgar, who waged war on these destructive animals, they were numerous in England, and an annual levy of 300 skins was imposed in Wales. It was long before they were exterminated; Nottinghamshire was infested in the reign of Henry VI, but they had disappeared from England by 1509. According to Surtees (vol. I, p. 109), the last wolf was killed in Scotland in 1682, but they are said to have existed in the North of Scotland up to 1743, while in Ireland they lingered for another twenty years. The name of the animal is preserved in Wolf Rock off Land's End; in the Irish wolfhound, used formerly for hunting wolves, which were especially numerous in the north of Ireland, in various plants, such as the aconite or wolf's bane, and the lupine; and in the disease known as lupus, so called from its destructive nature. No doubt such nursery tales as "Little Red Riding Hood" have an origin in stories told to frighten children, as the name of Napoleon, "Bony," was employed at the beginning of the last century.

Other so-called wolves, the maned wolf of South America, the coyote, the wolf of Abyssinia, the Cape hunting dog, the Aard wolf, and the dingo of Australia may be ignored for the purposes of this book; they are more wild dogs or jackals than wolves; the wild dog of India and the jackal, like all these animals, have not been known to attack human beings. I have in the Satpura Hills come upon a large pack of twenty or more red dogs, which have stood or moved about in an unconcerned manner at close quarters, but they showed no aggressive intentions, although this species has been known to attack tigers and leopards.

The wolf is more interesting and certainly more terrible in fiction than in fact. This may be owing to its existence as the only destructive animal in the greater part of Europe within historical times, a circumstance which has given rise to its frequency in story and legend, as well as in the popular superstitions of many countries. Wolves have always inspired man with dread. The Romans believed that if a wolf saw a man before the man saw the wolf, the man would be suddenly struck dumb, and unable to call for assistance. Yet it is at least doubtful whether a single wolf would attack a man. However, wolves were long ago known as man-eaters. Chaucer described the statue of Armipotent in the Temple of Mars—

> A wolfe there lay before him at his feete,
> With eyen red, and of a man he eat.

In appearance the Alsatian dogs now fashionable in England bear much resemblance in shape, in the cocked ears, and in coloration, to the wolf. Wolves have been known to breed with dogs, and in India hybrids have been recorded. In the Buldana district of Berar, where wolves were plentiful thirty years ago, a dog was observed going leisurely towards a flock of sheep, which took no notice of it. But soon an outcry from the shepherd attracted attention, and wolves were seen carrying off fragments of a sheep which they had seized and torn to pieces; the dog had been acting as leader of the pack. One of the wolves made for some bushes out of which three whelps came, one of which was captured, and proved to be a hybrid wolf-dog. This and other hybrids from the same pack became as domesticated as pariah dogs are in India, showing no signs of fear; one was shot. Wolves have been tamed; a story is related that a lady in Italy had a tame and affectionate wolf which followed her about like a dog. On her return from a few days' absence the animal jumped up and put his paws on her shoulders, and immediately fell dead, apparently from excess of joy.

It has been said that the Indian wolf is probably the same as the European animal, varying owing to geographical circumstances. I killed one in Baluchistan which differed in no way from those shot in the Deccan. The Indian wolf, like the European one, varies greatly in colour, some being brown or reddish brown, and some grey with more or less black in the fur. In Europe and in India they have much the same habits, although in Europe they are more forest dwellers, while in India they are found chiefly in scrub jungle, and not in the great forests. This, however, is what one would expect, for the European wolf has been obliged to seek seclusion from man in uncultivated tracts, while in India there are large areas of desert or of jungle interspersed with cultivation, where the wolves share the ground with the antelope, gazelle, hares and other game on which they chiefly prey. They are also, like the wolves of Europe, addicted to killing sheep, goats and dogs, and opportunity makes them more given to child-murder in India than in Europe. They attack with ferocity ; I have seen a pair seize a goat and, after a tug-of-war lasting a few moments, tear it to pieces and devour it. They will attack cattle and horses in Russia, creeping close up to the victim and seizing it by the muzzle, where they will hang on until the prey is exhausted, just as a bull-terrier will hang on to a bullock's nose. It is said that three cows or horses are able to keep off a wolf, by presenting their heels and kicking it, as a pony has been known to keep a lion off with its hoofs, and a buffalo to repel a leopard with its horns. Dr. Jerdon relates that a wolf joined his greyhounds in pursuit of a fox, and sat down at a distance to look on when the hounds were worrying their quarry.

Wolves in India often live in earths, generally made by porcupines, or in holes under rocks in ravines and hills. They are wary and difficult to approach, but on one occasion a wolf, which was probably gorged with food, came trotting along indifferent to my presence and lay down in a depression of the ground only some twenty yards off, where it was missed by a very bad shot. The sportsman often sees them stalking antelope and gazelle. When pursued they have a habit of stopping to gaze, and so offer a good shot. Usually they are silent, but I heard one utter a dog-like yelp when struck by a bullet.

In Russia they are hunted with dogs, and shot. Another method was said to be to drive over the snow with a young pig tethered behind the sledge, when its squeals would attract the wolves within shot. In India the natives used to dig a deep pit, concealed with leaves, suspending over it a kid in a basket; over this was hung a pot of water, having a small hole in it, through which a drop at a time fell on the kid to make it bleat; or a split coconut was affixed to the ear for the same purpose. The wolf would spring at the kid and fall into the pit.

It is related that Captain Richards of the Bengal Army had in his service a shikari who would enter the earths of wolves and hyenas, fasten thongs to their legs, and drag them out. He "had a sense of smell so acute that he could tell whether an earth was occupied, and whether by wolf or hyena, and this although his nose was depressed on a level with his cheeks."

It may be remarked, however, that this feat was not perhaps due to a sense of smell, although wild beasts smell strongly at close quarters; I have smelt a tiger in the jungle, and a leopard which I nearly trod on revealed its presence in a bush by the smell. But the tracks and hair at the entrance to the earths would reveal whether the animal was wolf or hyena, while the presence or absence of the hard-backed flies which infest these animals would show whether the beast was at home or not.

In extreme cold, as in exceptional winters in Russia, there is no doubt that wolves assemble in large packs and attack domesticated animals, horses drawing sledges, and even man himself. In the milder climates of Western Europe, in France and Germany, there are no such stories as come from Russia. In most winters sensational paragraphs of this kind appear in the popular press, but these are generally apocryphal tales, like those of eagles carrying off children which periodically reappear. I was told in White Russia, on the track of Napoleon's invasion, near Smolensk, where wolves were numerous, that they had never been known to attack people. No doubt the wounded stragglers of Napoleon's Grand Army in the retreat of 1812 suffered from wolves, but these were probably less cruel and persistent in their attacks than the Russian peasantry.

The stories of attacks by packs of wolves during the Russian winter, when snow covers the ground and when it freezes hard for many weeks, bear much resemblance to one another. But they are probably very rare occurrences. It is recorded, however, that 160 people were killed by wolves in Russia in the winter of 1875, when the animals were emboldened by hunger.

The tales of pursuit of travellers by wolves bear a generic likeness but vary in specific detail. Some of them may be true; some certainly are not.

It is related in *The Hunting Grounds of the Old World*,[1] the author of which was a good story-teller, that in Circassia in the winter of 1852 a party of eleven horsemen with five Russian prisoners, one a woman, were traversing a plain when they were followed by an immense horde of wolves. The nearest hamlet was seven miles off, but the horses were tired and with difficulty made their way through the snow. It was decided to sacrifice the prisoners one by one so that the Circassians might escape. Contrary to the usual custom of civilized peoples, the woman was the first to be thrown to the wolves, her horse being hamstrung, and rider and horse were soon devoured, while the party pressed on their way. But this morsel did not satisfy the pursuers, and the prisoners were sacrificed in turn. Even four Russians and their mounts did not satiate the taste for blood; two horses were then abandoned, "the riders drew their yataghans and, shouting their war-cry, died like men, fighting to the last." The survivors were now only two miles from safety, but more sacrifices were necessary, so an old Mahomedan, whose two sons were of the party, bade his comrades farewell, felled his horse with a blow from the butt of his pistol, and sacrificed himself to save the rest. The pack closely pursued the eight survivors, and escape seemed hopeless when the chief drew his pistol and shot through the head the nearest man to him who, however, though dead, kept his seat until a second

[1] By Major H. A. Leveson, the Old Shekarry, author of *Sport in Many Lands*.

shot brought corpse and horse to the ground. This checked the pursuit, the party gained the shelter of a hut, but in shutting the door left outside one of their comrades whose horse had lagged behind, and he and his steed were pulled down and devoured before their eyes. After this, the wolves long continued round the hut, but many were shot, for the party had plenty of ammunition, and, after devouring their dead companions, the wolves fled into the night.

This preposterous story may be compared with others representing a family of a dozen or so children travelling by sledge over the snow, pursued by wolves; one by one the spare horses were sacrificed, until, there being only one left to draw the sledge, the turn of the children came, and they were thrown to the wolves one at a time by the parent to enable the survivors to escape.

A story which bears the impress of truth was related by Mr. Hutchinson, an English resident in Russia, who, in the terrible winter of 1860–61, had to travel by sledge 30 miles from a town on the Volga to Yaroslav. In this town he had shot a wolf in the courtyard of his house the day before starting on his journey. Many reports were current as to the hunger and unusual boldness of the wolves, which were said even to have attacked a small village. Consequently the traveller was well armed with a six-chambered revolver, a nine-inch bear-knife, and a heavily weighted blackthorn cudgel. He was just about to start when a Russian neighbour came up and asked if he might join him for the journey; he was described as "the last man I should have chosen as a travelling-companion in a narrow sledge, for he weighed over twenty stone, had great difficulty in breathing, and when once he was seated, almost required horse-power to get him up again." The Russian rolled in and filled three-parts of the sledge; the driver gathered up the rope reins; Hutchinson jumped in, and off they went against a blinding drift.

The Russian observed the weapons and grunted in his own language: "Pistolet; volki; stryelyai; khorosho!" ("Pistol; wolves; shoot; good!")—for he spoke only in monosyllables. Asked whether he had any weapons, he replied "No," and relapsed into his corner when the bear-knife was handed to him. They had made only 10 miles in six hours on the track, which was obliterated by snow but indicated by trees at wide intervals, when the driver shouted, "Volki! volki!" Hutchinson sprang up and looking ahead saw six gaunt wolves sitting right in the way, a hundred yards off. The horses huddled themselves together, trembling in every limb and refusing to stir. The men shouted, but the wolves did not move. The fat Russian, gathering a handful of hay from the bottom of the sledge, rolled it into a ball and handed it to Hutchinson, saying: "Spichka!" ("A match!") Hutchinson set fire to the hay, and as it blazed, threw it among the wolves, the driver having lashed his horses to within a short distance of them. It worked like a charm. Instantly the wolves parted, three on each side, and skulked off at right angles, dragging their tails like beaten curs.

The horses went on at speed, the driver standing up and urging them on towards the post-house, a mile distant, with lash and voice. But Hutchinson, looking back as they turned a bend on the track, saw the pack following in swift pursuit. Throwing off his sheepskin coat, he sprang on to the front seat beside the driver, with his face to the enemy. The fat Russian sat still in his corner and neither moved nor spoke, but the bear-knife gleamed in his hand. The track became worse, the horses could not maintain their pace, the wolves ran beside the sledge, and in a drift the horses came to a walk, and the first wolf on Hutchinson's side made a dash at the horse next to him; the pistol was fired within a foot and a half of his head, and he fell shot through the brain. The Russian shouted "Bravo!" and the second shot shattered a leg of the next wolf, which dropped behind. But then the pistol fell into the sledge as, with a sudden jolt, the horses floundered into a deep drift; then they came to a dead stop, and there was a wolf at each side of the sledge, trying to get in.

Hutchinson with both hands brought the bludgeon down upon the head of the wolf on his side, and it tumbled over with its skull smashed in. As he stooped to pick up the pistol he was astonished to see his companion coolly thrust one of his arms into the other wolf's mouth, and as coolly with his disengaged hand draw the knife with a deep sharp cut across its throat. A peculiar cry among the horses drew his attention. Looking round he saw another wolf fastened on the off horse's neck. The driver, who was between him and the wolf, cried out: "Give me the pistol!" and in a moment the horse was free. The remaining wolf ran off, followed by the one with the broken leg; the wolf last shot was tumbling in the snow. The travellers reached Yaroslav without further adventure.

Wolves, either in Europe or in Asia, are not given to

attacking adult human beings except when driven by starvation in winters of extreme severity as in Russia, or occasionally in India. They are said to have surrounded and killed a party of 24 soldiers of the Grand Army during the retreat from Moscow in 1812, and probably the blood of wounded stragglers attracted their attacks in many instances. It is related in Forbes' *Oriental Memoirs* that during a terrible famine in 1785 "people crowded for relief to the cantonment at Cawnpore, and perishing from weakness before they could obtain it, filled up the ways with their dead bodies. This attracted the wolves, and being thus fleshed with human food, they considered the country as their own and man as their proper prey. They not only frequently carried off children, but actually attacked the sentries on their posts. Three of them attacked a sentinel, who, after shooting the first and bayoneting the second, was killed by the third. It was necessary to double the sentries. A man, his wife, and child, were sleeping in their hut; the mother was awakened by the shrieks of the child in her arms, a wolf had seized it by the leg and carried it off in spite of her struggles."

There was a severe famine in the Deccan in 1900, and there were numbers of human skulls to be seen strewn about the country. A small pack of wolves infested the neighbourhood of a village near Jalna, where they had earths under some rocks at the head of a ravine, from which we attempted in vain to dislodge them, but the nature of the ground made this impossible. The villagers declared that they had killed two female inhabitants of the hamlet.

In India they seldom attack grown men, but Mr. Sterndale mentions having heard of a woman being killed. In the Central Provinces wolves were at one time numerous, but are said to be seldom seen now, although I commonly came across them in Berar forty years ago, when a child was brought into hospital at Ellichpur, with its throat torn by a wolf. Twenty years before that, Captain Forsyth saw parties of five or six, and found them carrying off children, but he said that only when confirmed in the habit of man-eating did they attack, at an advantage, full-grown women and even adult men. Many instances occurred during the construction of the railway through the low jungles north of Jabalpur, of labourers on the works being so attacked, and sometimes killed and eaten. "The attack was commonly made by a pair of wolves, one of which seized the victim by the neck from behind, preventing outcry, while the other, coming swiftly up, tore out the entrails in front." These confirmed man-eaters were exceedingly wary, and said to be fully able to discriminate between a helpless victim and an armed man.

In 1878 nearly 900 people were killed by wolves, over 600 of these in what are now known as the United Provinces. They also killed over 10,000 cattle. The human victims were no doubt mainly children. In 1900 the human victims in the United Provinces had fallen to 285; but in that year wolves killed 42 people in the Raipur District of the Central Provinces, which may be compared with 220 for the whole of those provinces in 1878. It is possible that at the earlier date more of these deaths were due to female infanticide, wolves being indicated as the culprits.

Captain Forsyth relates that when marching through the Damoh District he heard that for months past a pair of wolves had carried off a child every few days from the centre of a village in broad daylight. The inhabitants had made no attempt whatever to kill them, although their haunts were well known, and lay not a quarter of a mile from the village. Only to propitiate the goddess Devi, a shapeless stone under a tree had been daubed with vermilion and offered rice and coconuts. The wolves behaved in a manner characteristic of the tactics of these animals in seeking their prey. The village was on the slope of a hill at the foot of which ran the bed of a stream thickly fringed with grass and bushes. "The main street of the village, where children were always at play, ran down the slope of the hill; and while one of the wolves, which was smaller than the other, would ensconce itself among some low bushes between the village and the bottom of the hill, the other would go round to the top, and, watching an opportunity, race down through the street, picking up a child by the way, and making off with it to the thick cover in the nullah." At first people used to pursue, and sometimes made the marauder drop his prey; but in the confusion the companion wolf would seize another child, while the first was usually injured beyond recovery, so that there were two victims instead of one.

An infant a few years old had been carried off on the morning of Captain Forsyth's arrival, but such is the character of these Hindus that not only had they never made any attempt to rid themselves of these monsters, but he could not at first get beaters to drive the wolves out of cover. At length he obtained a few village outcasts, and beat out and shot the wolves. He described them as "evidently mother and son; the latter about three-quarters grown, with a reddish-yellow, well-furred coat and plump appearance; the mother, a lean and grizzled hag, with hideous pendent dugs, and slaver dropping from her disgusting jaws." Their lairs in the grass were filled with fragments of bones.

Early in 1890 and 1891 a pack of wolves killed 23 persons and wounded 20 in the Narsinghpur District of the Central Provinces, and killed 95 people in the adjoining Hoshangabad District. A campaign for their destruction was undertaken by Mr. Playfair, District Superintendent of Police, who destroyed 7 wolves and 10 cubs; 13 large wolves and 23 cubs had been killed before he began operations, and the whole pack was thus "liquidated." When this pack first appeared, goats and ponies formed their staple food; they usually lay out in the open fields or in patches of jungle, and they could be driven off by young children. They later took to devouring children, but my recollection is that they afterwards began attacking adults; the number of wounded points to this, for children would be unlikely to survive attack. It was said that they began man-eating after feeding on insufficiently buried corpses. These events seem to have led to the extermination of wolves in the Central Provinces.

Packs of pariah dogs, such as infest towns and villages in India, and used to roam the streets of Stamboul, have been known to behave like wolves. At Jalandar, in the Punjab, fifty years ago, a boy threw a stone at a dog. The dog flew at him; other dogs joined in, and the boy was overpowered, torn to pieces, and eaten.

CHAPTER XVI

WOLF-CHILDREN AND WERE-WOLVES

CLOSELY connected with the child-stealing propensities of wolves are the stories of children popularly supposed to have been brought up by these animals, and immortalized in *The Jungle Book*. The wolf-children, however, have not the intelligence of Mowgli, unless we accept the mythical Romulus and Remus; they have all been idiots. In modern times we do not hear of them in Europe, although a number have been reported in India; but the conditions of European life do not generally tend to favour the abandonment of children in the wilds, although we might expect to hear such tales from Russia.

Shakespeare knew of these traditions, for in *A Winter's Tale* Antigonus conjures the spirits:

> Come on, poor babe:
> Some powerful spirit instruct the kites and ravens
> To be thy nurses! Wolves and bears, they say,
> Casting their savageness aside have done
> Like offices of pity.

Tradition in the pages of Firdusi relates that the son of a Persian general was exposed on Mount Elburz and brought up by beasts of prey; and we read of a Phrygian boy being nourished by an eagle. Semiramis, the founder of the Assyrian empire of Nineveh, was reputed to have been fed by doves, a story that has a Biblical flavour. Wild men have been reported in Europe, such as the one discovered by shepherds in the Pyrenees in 1774, and Peter the Wild Boy, found in the forest of Hertzwold in Hanover, who was brought to England and buried at Northchurch in 1785, as recorded in an inscription beneath a sketch by Bartolozzi on a brass plate in the parish church.

In India the North-West Provinces and Oudh were the particular abode of the wolf-children, of whom so much has been heard since the time when, in 1850, Sir William Sleeman recorded supposed instances of their occurrence.[1] The subject is, however, more complicated than appears on the surface, and is probably closely connected with superstition and crime. It is remarkable that practically all these stories come from one province. Wolves were perhaps more numerous in Oudh than in other provinces of India, but they were abundant in many parts of the country. Their prevalence may be illustrated by the statistics of the destruction of human life by wolves and of the numbers of wolves killed in 1878. In that year in the North-West Provinces and Oudh 624 human beings were killed, and 2589 wolves were destroyed; in the Punjab the figures were respectively 14 human beings and 1120 wolves; in Bengal 152 and 919; and in the Central Provinces 32 and 219. In 1900 the human victims of wolves in the United Provinces were only 285.

These figures are significant. For example, in the North-West Provinces and Oudh, now known as the

[1] *A Journey Through the Kingdom of Oude*. By Major-General Sir William Sleeman. Bentley, 1858.

United Provinces, the mortality ascribed to wolves is out of all proportion to similar figures for the Punjab. The causes of this discrepancy are worth investigation, although these must be quite conjectural. But the figures seem to indicate remarkable and improbable variation in the character of wolves in the different provinces. The causes must be sought elsewhere.

In the preceding chapter it was related how Captain Forsyth destroyed two wolves that lived almost in the precincts of a village in the Central Provinces, preying on the children of the inhabitants. He ascribed the immunity of the wolves to apathy, and was evidently unaware of the Hindu superstition that the family of a man who kills a wolf, or even wounds it, soon meets with disaster. There is also a superstition that the community of a village within the boundaries of which a a wolf has been killed or a drop of its blood has fallen is doomed to destruction. Sir William Sleeman wrote in 1850 that the Rajputs of Oudh were already beginning to abandon this superstition, which has perhaps now disappeared. But in the late 'sixties, in Forsyth's day, it was, no doubt, still prevalent in remoter places. Hindus dare not destroy a wolf, even though it may have eaten their own children or have one in its mouth. It is not surprising, then, that the villagers took no steps to free themselves from the wolves, and that Forsyth could get no assistance for this purpose except from the lowest outcasts, who are made to live in a separate community outside the village, and who are free from the rigours of Hindu customs and beliefs. The inhabitants had no objection to the destruction of wolves outside their boundaries by other people. But the terrible depredations committed with impunity

Previous to the annexation of Oudh and other provinces, can be partly accounted for in this manner.

It is also possible that female infanticide, so prevalent one time, especially in Oudh, was responsible for many deaths ascribed to wolves, which were made to fear some of the blame of that custom. This may, perhaps, account for the small proportion of human beings killed by wolves in the Punjab, where the inhabitants are largely Mahomedan and Sikh, in comparison with the mortality attributed to the same cause in the Rajput Provinces. It is unfortunate that the proportions of the sexes of victims of wolves are not recorded, for they might have thrown some light on this theory. Perhaps also the murder of children for the sake of the gold and silver ornaments with which the parents deck their offspring of both sexes accounts for some of these victims of "wolves." The tragedy of a child seized and carried off by a wolf is not generally witnessed by the parents, for wolves, like other man-eaters, usually hunt by stealth; nor is a child murdered before witnesses. Such murders are mostly the work of vagrant criminal classes, just those people who used to make a living by collecting ornaments belonging to the victims of wolves in the dens of these animals. They would be ready to act the part of wolf also in order to secure their booty, and it is quite possible that such murders might increase as the source of revenue from the victims of wolves diminished owing to the extermination or reduction of those animals. Numbers of children used to be murdered every day in India for the sake of their ornaments, and such deaths might well be ascribed to wolves.

Not the least of the blessings of British rule in India

is the reduction of female infanticide and child murder, and the destruction of wolves where people had not the will, even if they possessed the means, to destroy them. In the same category was the suppression of the Thugs who infested the highways and strangled whole parties of travellers, and of the Pindaris and other gang robbers who formerly ravaged the country and would hack off the limbs of children as the easiest way of getting their bracelets and anklets.

The chief evidence for the occurrence of children carried off and nurtured by or in the company of wolves rests on investigations made by Sir William Sleeman in 1849. There are also the records of the Sikandra Orphanage near Agra, where so-called "wolf-children" have been sheltered. A typical instance recorded by Sir William Sleeman is that of a boy alleged to have been found in 1847 in a den with wolves near Chandur, about ten miles from Sultanpur. He then appeared to be about nine years old. It is related that a trooper sent on duty to Chandur was passing along the bank of the river about noon when he saw a large wolf leave her den followed by three cubs and a little boy. They drank at the river, while the trooper sat on his horse watching them. When they turned back, the trooper tried to cut the boy off, but he ran as fast as the cubs, and as the ground was uneven they got away into the den. The trooper then got people with pick-axes from Chandur, and they dug down six or eight feet, when the wolf party bolted. They were pursued and the boy was secured. On the way to the village he struggled and tried hard to rush into every den they came near. He could not speak, but only growl or snarl. He was afraid of grown-up people, but would rush and snarl at a child and try to bite it. He rejected cooked meat, but ate raw flesh with avidity, holding it under his paws on the ground like a dog; he had no objection to dogs eating with him, and made special friends with one.

The boy was sent to Captain Nicholetts, at Sultanpur, by the Raja of Hasnapur, who saw him when the trooper brought him in, and from whose report this account was taken. Nicholetts' servants took care of him. He would not keep on any clothing, even in the coldest weather, and when a stuffed cotton quilt was given to him, he tore it to pieces and ate it with his daily bread. He ate anything, but preferred raw meat and bones, and he ate earth and small stones. His features were coarse, his countenance repulsive, and his habits filthy. He would run to his food on all-fours. He formed no attachment, but would sit and stroke his dog friend, but did not care when it was shot. Captain Nicholetts believed that the parents recognised the boy when found, but, finding him stupid and insensible, they left him to charity. He was quiet and required no restraint. He used signs, pointing to his mouth when hungry. He was never heard to speak until a few minutes before his death in August 1850, when he put his hands to his head, said it ached, and asked for water, which he drank, and then died.

In another case the story of the capture of an alleged wolf-boy near Chupra bears so much resemblance to the preceding one that except for the dates it seems to be almost identical. There is, however, an earlier history of this boy which itself indicates a similarity with Captain Nicholetts' remark regarding the parents of the first child. In March 1843 a cultivator of Chupra with his wife and little boy of three went to work in his field. The child had a mark from a scald on the left knee. A wolf suddenly rushed from behind a bush, caught the boy up by the loins and made off with him; the mother followed screaming, and people from the village ran to help, but they soon lost sight of the wolf and its prey. Six years afterwards, two sepoys came from Singramau, which is 10 miles from Chupra, on the bank of the Khobai rivulet. While they sat on the border of the jungle, watching for hogs, they saw three wolf-cubs and a boy go down to the stream to drink. The sepoys ran after them when they made for a den in a ravine and caught the boy, who was angry and ferocious, bit at them, and seized the barrel of a gun in his teeth. They took him home, fed him on raw flesh of hares and birds, and let him go in the bazaar of Kolipur to be fed on charity. Here a man from Chupra saw him, and told his neighbours, and the bereaved mother, having been given a description of him, went to see him, recognized the scar on the knee, and discovered also a birth-mark on his thigh, and saw the marks of the wolf's teeth on his loins. She took him home with her, and his habits of eating and general behaviour resembled those of the preceding case.

The Raja of Hasnapur mentioned another lad who came to the town, and "who had evidently been brought up by wolves." He had short hair all over his body when he first came, but this by degrees disappeared when he was given salt with his food. He walked upright, and could be made to understand signs, but could not talk. Several similar cases were recorded by Sir William Sleeman, all on native hearsay, and in all of which troopers, or sepoys, a she-wolf, and two or three wolf-cubs figure. In fact, they bear a generic resemblance to one another which points to a common origin, probably traditional. In one instance, at Bundi, it was related that one night, when the wolf-boy was lying under a tree, two wolves were seen to come up to him stealthily and smell him. They then touched him, and he got up and put his hands on their heads, and they began to play with him, capering round while he threw straw and leaves at them. Next night three wolves came, and a few nights afterwards four. They came four or five times and played together. It was thought by the spectator, who had adopted the boy, that the first two were the cubs that were with him when he was caught, and that they were prevented from seizing him by recognizing the smell, which is very probable, for we are told that this was "very offensive"! In this case the usual mother turned up, the usual marks were recognized, this time on the head and chest. This boy, like others, went about on all-fours, having callosities on the hands and feet from this mode of progression, and he ate raw flesh and tore off trousers when they were put on him. Those concerned in these things told Sir William Sleeman that they were strictly true. Sleeman remarks that "it is remarkable that he could discover no well-authenticated instance of a man who had been nurtured in a wolf's den having been found"; and that, as many boys had been recovered after they had been many years with wolves, they must either die or be destroyed by wolves or other wild animals before they attain manhood.

To come to more recent times, Mr. Valentine Ball,[1] a very competent observer, visited the Sikandra

[1] *Jungle Life in India.* By Valentine Ball, M.A. De la Rue, 1880.

Orphanage in 1874, and saw a wolf-boy, the survivor of two who had been there. Mr. Erhardt, the Superintendent, said there was an elderly fellow in the Lucknow madhouse who had been "dug out of a wolf's den by a European doctor," when, he forgot, but a number of years ago. He added that "the facility with which the boys get along on their four feet (hands and feet) is surprising." Before eating or tasting food they smelt it, as do many children, and when they didn't like the smell they rejected it, as most of us do!

The boy whom Ball examined was led in by the hand; he "presented an appearance not uncommonly seen in ordinary idiots." His forehead was low, his teeth prominent, his manner restless. He grinned in a way more simian than human. He depended more upon smell than taste for the identification of objects. He was slender, 5 feet 3 inches in height, about fifteen years old, and had been nine years at the orphanage. He was of a happy temperament. His arms were remarkably short, about nineteen and a half inches, probably due to his having gone on all-fours. The Superintendent was not in charge of the Orphanage when he came, but a native guide in Agra said that he was in a magistrate's court when this boy, the body of an old she-wolf, and two cubs were brought in. For some time he was kept by the Civil Surgeon, bound to a charpoy or native bedstead in order to straighten his legs, and several months passed before he was able to maintain an erect position. This is an early example of orthopædic surgery which should delight the heart of Sir Robert Armstrong Jones!

If these idiot children were found with wolves, they

must have been taken to the wolves' dens uninjured, and perhaps owing to there being already sufficient food, they took their place with the cubs, or they may have been taken in to suckle by a she-wolf who had been deprived of her cubs. Ball asked "an eminent surgeon, who formerly resided in Oudh" (perhaps Sir Joseph Fayrer ?), what he thought of these stories, and his reply was: "I don't believe one of them." A number of letters relating to this subject appeared in *The Times* in April 1927, including one from Sir John Hewett, who saw the boy in the Sikandra Orphanage in the same year that Ball saw him. Sir John relates that a generation later, when he was Lieutenant-Governor of Agra and Oudh, he visited the Orphanage and was told by the Father in charge that the boy had grown up to manhood and lived to between thirty and forty years of age. He never spoke, but associated very much with another inmate. When the latter died he showed great emotion, and had constantly pointed to the skies at the funeral. This action had, perhaps, been taught, for the Rev. Mr. W. McLean, who saw this wolf-boy, named Sanichar, or Saturday, from the day of his capture, when he was dying, and who conducted his funeral, says that he would close his eyes and point upwards, to indicate the passing from life.

It is remarkable that nearly all the cases recorded are males, and from one province. However, one correspondent of *The Times* wrote of an Indian Christian priest who in 1926 had in his charge a girl of about twelve, who, four years before had been dug out of a wolf's den, had become fairly human in her habits, and spoke a few words; and two cases, in which the sex is not stated, are said to have occurred in the Santal Perganas, or in Chota Nagpur in 1925. Mr. Broun, I.C.S., tells of two alleged wolf-boys of about ten who were brought to him in 1895. They were "extremely emaciated and idiotic-looking, unable to speak, and making only uncouth noises, having callosities on hands and knees. They tore up food like wild beasts." Mr. Broun adds that enquiries were made, and there was no reason to doubt that the story of their being found in a wolf's den was probable. At the same time it is not said whether they were found in company with wolves, or were derelicts. The last recorded case, which gave rise to *The Times* correspondence, beginning with the present writer's article in that paper on April 8th, 1927, was the discovery of a boy near Mianwana at that time, and reported in the *Pioneer* of Allahabad. Marks of this boy had been found in a wolf's den near which he was captured, but there was no suggestion that he had been suckled by wolves.

The case for wolf-children rests on such slender grounds that, but for the respect due to Sir William Sleeman, it would be rejected at once. There have been no first-hand European witnesses, for the "European doctor" mentioned in one case is only vaguely spoken of. The instances are almost entirely confined to a province where superstitions of the wolf are or were especially prevalent, as they used to be in Europe and still are in Russia. Why do we not hear of them from the Punjab, or Bengal, or the Central Provinces, where wolves were abundant and predatory, as shown by the mortality figures, but where they seem to have no predilection for adopting the children of men?

The combination of circumstances necessary to produce a "wolf-child" must be so rare as to be infinitesimal, yet the alleged instances are numerous. The infant would have to be a suckling, or very small, and would have to survive the attack of a savage beast "bloody with ravin," which generally inflicts immediate death. Such attack is well described in an article in the Allahabad *Pioneer* of November 25th, 1874: "Night comes on, the wolf slinks about the village site, marking the unguarded hut. It comes to one protected by a low wall, or closed by an ill-fitting mat. Inside, the mother, wearied by the long day's work, is asleep with her child in her arms, unconscious of the danger at hand. The wolf makes its spring fastens its teeth in the baby's throat, slings the little body across its back, and is off before the mother is fully aware of her loss. Pursuit is generally useless. If forced to drop its burden the cruel creature tears it beyond power of healing, while should it elude pursuit, the morning's search results in the discovery of a few bones, the remnants of the dreadful meal." Those who have seen the ferocious onslaught of a wolf will scarcely believe that it can be survived by a tender infant. And if it survived the attack it would have to survive the dangers of the den. In India, in times of famine, children were often abandoned or lost in the jungle, or idiots or others might wander from their homes, and some of the instances of wolf-children recorded may belong to that category, while all probably have in their history the mythical element.

We may leave Romulus and Remus to our classical scholars, who will also choose between Ovid and Pliny regarding Lycaon, the were-wolf. A more sinister aspect attaches to the superstition of were-wolves than to the stories of wolf-children. This dates from the earliest times, and is as old as Homer, although Pliny rejects Ovid's description of Lycaon, who was changed into a wolf as a punishment for his crimes. But the were-wolf is supposed to be the human being who has the power of assuming the form of a beast of prey. The beast tends to be the principal carnivorous animal in the country concerned—in Russia and Western Europe, a wolf; in Northern Europe, a bear; in Africa, a hyena or leopard, for the lion is apparently above such metamorphoses; and in India and the East, a tiger or leopard.

Olaus Magnus, the learned Archbishop of Upsal, who should have known better, says that were-wolves, transformed from men, were to be found in great abundance in the northern countries. "They enter beer-cellars and will drink up many barrels of beer; and then will pile up the empty barrels one on the top of the other in the middle of the cellar, in which particular they differ from natural wolves." Certainly they did not differ from natural men, and probably possessed only two legs apiece. In remote parts of Russia the peasantry believe in were-wolves, and a story is related of a nobleman, who said that when out in quest of game he was attacked by a fierce wolf which he put to flight after cutting off one of its paws. Returning to his castle he found that the paw had changed into a human hand, which he recognized from the rings as being that of his wife. The unfortunate lady was discovered to have had one hand cut off, and, being found guilty, was burnt at the stake as a were-wolf. No doubt the nobleman was in truth a scoundrel who exploited a prevailing superstition in order to get rid of his wife. Perhaps divorce was not as easy in those days as in our time.

It is a curious circumstance that, while old writers very naturally averred that the were-wolf had no tail, the same superstition prevails in India with regard to man-eating leopards, one of which I shot forty years ago. This animal was said to be black and tailless, doubtless because it was supposed to be a human being in the form of a beast of prey; but it was a normal leopard with the usual tail. Similar stories were prevalent regarding an unidentified animal which appeared in the Orel Government of Russia when I was in that country in 1893, where it attacked many people and killed some. An account of this beast appeared in *The Field* of December 9th, 1893. I had no opportunity of inspecting the tracks, but it may have been a wolf or possibly a panther escaped from a menagerie. It was too far north to have wandered from the Caucasus.

In 1521 three were-wolves, called *loups-garous*, were burned in France for having murdered several people with knives. One wonders why they did not use their teeth. The superstition was rife in some parts of France in comparatively recent times. In 1804 the inhabitants of Longeville were terribly annoyed by one of these monsters. Terrified by the supernatural character ascribed to it, the unfortunate villagers allowed themselves to be robbed and maltreated by this villainous animal during upwards of three years. At last, a young peasant, whose sweetheart had been cruelly outraged, lay in wait for the monster, armed with a gun, and fired a charge of buckshot into it, whereupon it stood up and was found to be an escaped convict.

Many were-wolves were no doubt persons suffering from the form of insanity known as lycanthropy. In 1598, in a wild and unfrequented spot near Cande, some countrymen came one day upon the mutilated corpse of a boy. As they approached, two wolves, which had been rending the body, bounded away into a thicket. The men gave chase, following upon the bloodstained tracks until they lost them, when suddenly they found a man half naked, with long hair and beard, and his hands dyed with blood, crouching among the bushes, his teeth chattering with fear. The man confessed to having killed and devoured the boy, and declared that he was able to transform himself into a wolf by means of a salve his parents had given him. The superstition very probably originated in the existence of such murderers as Dumollard, Jack the Ripper, Landru, Peter Kürten, and other perpetrators of crimes well known to alienists, which will be in the recollection of many.

A story remarkably similar to the last is related by Captain Forsyth in his *Highlands of Central India*, regarding a man-eating panther, which the aboriginal Gonds supposed to be a man in the form of the monster. A man and his wife met a panther on the road. The woman was terrified, but the man said: "Fear not; I possess a charm by means of which I can transform myself into any shape. I will now become a panther and remove this animal from the road, and on my return you must put this powder in my mouth, when I shall recover my proper shape." He handed his wife a powder, and swallowed another, and assuming the likeness of a panther, persuaded the animal to leave the path. Returning to the woman, he opened his mouth to receive the transforming charm ; but she, terrified by his dreadful appearance and open jaws, dropped it in the mire, and it was lost. Then in despair he killed the author of his misfortune, and became a man-eater to avenge himself on the race whose form he could never resume.

Stories of children being nurtured by wild animals are not confined to wolves. The hill-people of the Himalayas believe that bears adopt children, but it is not clear where Shakespeare got the idea in *A Winter's Tale*. A curious incident is related in the *Gentleman's Recreation*, by Nicholas Cox, printed in London in 1721, in a section on bear-hunting. The narrative is as follows : "There is a strange Report in History (if it be true) that in the mountains of Savoy a Bear carried a young Maid into his Den by violence . . . and while he kept her in his Den, he daily went forth and brought her the best Fruits he could get, presenting them to her as Food, as courtly as he could do it; but always when he went to forrage, he rolled a very great stone to the mouth of his Den, that the Virgin should not make her escape from him. At length her Parents, with long search, found their Daughter in the Bear's Den, who delivered her from that bestial Captivity."

Some years ago a case was reported from the Cachar Hills, in North-East India, of the adoption of an infant by a leopard who had lost her cub. The leopard was killed and the boy was delivered to the parents, who, as is usual in such cases, recognized him from marks or scars. When captured he bit anyone who touched him, and he would kill fowls that came within his reach. From running about on all-fours he had the callosities which come from this habit, but in course of time he learnt to walk upright.

From Africa we get stories of women being carried off into captivity by gorillas and chimpanzees, and from the Himalayas tales of children living with monkeys. The following description of such a case appeared in an Indian paper, where it was said that "considerable excitement had been caused in Naini Tal, by the arrival at the hospital of a wild-looking creature caught in the jungles and made over to the police. This creature was at one time beyond doubt a human female child, but is now best described as a female monkey-child of probably eight or nine years of age. But for the fact that the hospital authorities have cut the long shaggy hair from its head, and put on some clothes, and tied it by a rope to a pillar of the porch, it is at present in the same condition as when captured. It is suffering from an ulcerated foot, which has been bandaged since its arrival at the hospital, but this injury was probably the cause of its being unable to evade capture. When first brought in it was in a very frightened state, and would eat nothing but grass and raw potatoes, but later took bread and milk. It cried and whimpered, but is unable to talk, though it can undoubtedly hear. Its fear has now subsided to a great extent, and it will take and eat flour cakes and apples.

"That it was at one time a human child is proved beyond doubt by the fact that it carries vaccination marks on both arms, but its exposure to the elements has caused a thick growth of hair down each side of its face and down its spine. On its head are two or three heavy scars ; there are some circular scars on its knees, and two or three other places. There can be little doubt that it has always walked upright, as its elbows, knees, and hands show no signs of continual contact with the earth. Its hands are long, thin, and bony, and its nails long and strong. This is undoubtedly a case of a child abandoned, which is by no means uncommon during periods of scarcity in India. Of its survival in spite of adverse circumstances, of its partial return to the origin of man, and of the problem of how the child existed during the period it has lived in the jungles, unfortunately there are no means of telling, or how long it has lived there as the years of scarcity have been common of late."

CHAPTER XVII

BEARS

BEARS should strictly have no place in a history of man-eating animals, for although they are carnivorous and are accounted dangerous game, they are not addicted to preying on human beings. I can find only one record of the bear as man-eater, although there have been many man-killers, especially in the case of the Sloth Bear (*Ursus Labiatus*) of the Indian plains and lower ranges, and the Himalayan Black Bear (*U. torquatus*), which inhabits the whole range, including the offshoots of the Hindu Khush, and extending eastwards to Burma. Both these bears are black, and both have a large white horse-shoe mark on the chest. The only authentic instance of a bear eating human flesh is related in Mr. Dunbar-Brander's *Wild Animals in Central India*, where that authority on the habits of wild beasts says that for six weeks a sloth bear and two almost full-grown cubs were the terror of a jungle tract in Chanda, a district of the Central Provinces. It was definitely stated that on more than one occasion parts of the victims were eaten. But even in these cases it is most improbable that the people were killed for food after the manner of the great cats.

The legendary children of the Old Testament were killed by bears, no doubt of the brown Syrian species, because they called out "bald head" after an old man; but it is not stated that they were devoured. But although bears do not eat men, they have killed many. That is, however, no excuse for the appearance of Bruin in these pages. The bear is generally an attractive and harmless animal, and it is only fair that he should be given a chance to retrieve the aspersions that have been cast on his character, especially in America. Thus the naturalist Ord, who named or misnamed the grizzly (or was it originally "grisly"?) *Ursus horribilis*, for there is nothing horrible about the animal, in 1815 quoted in Guthrie's Geography from information contained in Lewis and Clark's Journal: "This animal is the monarch of the country he inhabits. The African lion or the tiger of Bengal is not more terrible or fierce. He is the enemy of man, and literally thirsts for human blood. So far from shunning, he seldom fails to attack and even to hunt him. The Indians make war upon these ferocious monsters with the same ceremonies as they do upon a tribe of their own species, and, in the recital of their victories, the death of one of them gives the warrior greater renown than the scalp of a human enemy. He possesses an amazing strength, and attacks without hesitation and tears to pieces the largest buffalo. The colour is usually such as the name indicates, although there are varieties from black to silvery whiteness. In shape he differs from the common black bear in being more long and lank. He does not climb trees, a circumstance which enables hunters, when attacked, to make their escape."[1]

For this unmerited character of bears the early

[1] *The Grizzly Bear.* By W. H. Wright. Werner Lawrie.

hunters are not wholly to blame, and this description is not justified by the journals on which it is based. No doubt some early hunters were prone to exaggerate, and their stories did not lose in being passed on from mouth to mouth, while they were reproduced with additions in works of natural history and fiction, such as the tales of Fenimore Cooper and Mayne Reid which delighted our childhood. The tradition of the ferocity of wild animals is long-lived and dies hard. Many who know that bears are not partial to human flesh firmly believe in the ferocity of the whole hairy tribe; they are popularly supposed to "hug" people, not in a loving embrace, although in the old days one might see tame bears in Russia and even in England doing this, but in order to squeeze all the breath out of their bodies. To the ignorant every tiger and lion is a man-eater, and every bear is ready to get up on its hind-legs and hug to death the first human being it meets with.

Wounded bears often show fight when followed up. According to Adams, a famous American hunter, naturalist, and bear-tamer of the first half of the last century, who seems to have read Guthrie, "the grizzly bear is the monarch of American beasts, and in many respects the most formidable animal in the world to be encountered. In comparison with the lion of Africa and the tiger of Asia, though these may exhibit more activity and bloodthirstiness, the grizzly is not second in courage, and excels them in power. Like the regions which he inhabits, there is a vastness in his strength which makes him a fit companion for the monster trees and rocks of the Sierras, and places him, if not the first, at least in the first rank of all quadrupeds."

It is certainly true that an animal weighing up to 1000 pounds exceeds in mass a lion or tiger of half that weight, but in velocity of movement and ferocity in attack it cannot be compared with the great felines which Adams had never seen, or had seen only behind the bars of a cage. If he had witnessed the charge of a wounded tiger or lion he would probably have changed his opinion. Although the great cats do not generally climb trees, that is seldom "a circumstance which enables hunters, when attacked, to make their escape." Their activity and power of concealment are infinitely greater than those of any bear. But it is natural that in a continent where there are no really dangerous animals, much should be made of a beast of such great size and strength as the grizzly. It is said to attain a length of over nine feet, but the American system of measurement is from the toe or claw of the fore-foot to the extremity of the opposite hind-foot. A skin thus measured was 9 feet 3 inches in length. A Kashmir brown bear's skin in my possession, measured in the same manner, is 8 feet 6 inches; the bear was 7 feet 4 inches long from nose to tail when shot.

The nearest record of a grizzly bear approximating to man-eating is described in Godman's *Natural History*, where it is related that two cubs when first received in the menagerie of the Philadelphia Museum were quite small, but speedily gave indications of that ferocity for which this species is so remarkable. "As they increased in size they became exceedingly dangerous, seizing and tearing to pieces every animal they could lay hold of, and expressing great eagerness to get at those accidentally brought within sight of their cage by grasping the iron bars with their paws and shaking them violently, to the terror of spectators, who felt insecure while witnessing such displays of their strength. In one instance an unfortunate monkey was walking over the top of their cage, when the end of the chain which hung from his waist dropped through within reach of the bears; they immediately seized it, dragged the screaming animal through the narrow aperture, tore him limb from limb, and devoured his mangled carcass almost instantaneously. At another time a small monkey thrust his arm through an opening in the bear-cage to reach after some object; one of them immediately seized him and with a sudden jerk tore the whole arm and shoulder-blade from the body and devoured it before anyone could interfere. They were still cubs and very little more than half-grown when their ferocity became so alarming as to excite continual apprehension lest they should escape, and they were killed to prevent such an event." No doubt a human being would have been similarly treated. But these animals were not under natural conditions, and in many cases grizzly bears have been tamed, especially by John Capen Adams, who was seen passing through the streets of San Francisco followed by a troupe of his grizzly bears, paying no attention to yelping dogs and a crowd of children who followed them. Bears in the Yellowstone National Park are tame and harmless. In a cage they may have been teased and may become ill-tempered. I have seen a man's arm seized by a caged sloth bear and stripped of flesh.

The early hunters were armed with weapons that were inefficient in comparison with modern rifles; to kill such big-game they had to go on pumping lead from small-bore, muzzle-loading fire-arms, charged with a light projectile and a small load of powder, into the immense bodies of the bears; it is not surprising that an animal harried in this way often turned on its aggressors, who had to get to closer quarters with it than is necessary with the long-ranging weapons of to-day. Then they started with preconceived notions of the character of the animal, imparted by Indians who, armed only with bows and arrows and tomahawks, found the grizzly a formidable beast to attack; and its imposing appearance added to the effect. Sir Alexander Mackenzie, who explored the Peace River in 1795 and saw bears' tracks 9 inches wide, said that "the Indians entertain great apprehension of this kind of bear, which is called the grisly bear, and they never venture to attack it except in a party of three or four." He never saw a grizzly.

Messrs. Lewis and Clark, who, in 1805, were the first white men to meet with the animal on the Upper Missouri, recorded in their journals accounts of the hunting of these creatures, and these formed the basis of subsequent ideas and traditions. They had many narrow escapes from wounded bears, but they did not often find them aggressive until they were attacked. Once a man carrying some meat was pursued, the smell of the meat perhaps being attractive. On one occasion a bear carried off some buffalo meat near their camp, but did not molest them. They did not perhaps exaggerate, but their descriptions gave rise to exaggeration in the minds of those who followed them. Thus W. H. Wright says that he started on his first bear-hunt with the idea that "all that was necessary was to go to the hills, let one's scent blow down breeze, and then shoot the ferocious animals that worked their way up-wind with the intention of eating you." He naturally did not get a grizzly for some time, these animals, like other bears, having a very keen scent, and bolting when they get a whiff of the smell of man, as I have seen them do at a distance of a quarter of a mile in the Himalayas. But at length he realized that the bear stories he had heard "were just stories." He gives in his book an excellent account of these animals, and those who wish to learn all about the same mild-tempered beast in Alaska cannot do better than read the more recent work of Mr. Holzworth.

The brown bear is found generally throughout mountainous regions in Europe, although it has disappeared from many parts of the Alps and other ranges where it was once abundant. It is common in the plains of Russia, and is said to inhabit the Atlas Mountains of Morocco. There seems to be little difference between the grizzly of America and the European and Asiatic animal, although there are considerable variations in size. All have much the same character; they are in general mild animals, and do not molest man so long as they are not attacked. In Russia they live in forests, in the Himalayas they are found on more open ground. They were common in Kashmir forty years ago, seldom descending below a height of some 7000 feet, and hibernating in winter. It is often said that these bears have a large accumulation of fat when they go into hibernation, and that they emerge in spring in bad condition, but one that had only recently emerged from its winter quarters, and was shot in the snow in Kashmir on the 23rd April, was very fat and had a splendid coat.

In Russia bears are tracked to their lairs, called

berloga, when they retreat to hibernate, generally on the first fall of snow, and the peasants who track them to their winter quarters sell the secret of their position according to the weight of the bear. Near Vitebsk I drove 50 miles over the snow to a forest where bears were said to be located and stayed in a hut. Next day a hundred or more peasants assembled, and we beat a considerable extent of forest, but saw nothing more interesting than the tracks of a lynx. It was said that no one in the district had ever been hurt by bears. In the Himalayas this bear has occasionally knocked down and clawed a man, but probably in a rush to escape rather than with aggressive intention. They sometimes rob sheepfolds, and feed on carrion. The Himalayan isabelline bear has a habit of eating the carcasses of ibex and other animals overwhelmed by avalanches and exposed when the snow melts. A bear one night entered a village near my camp in Kashmir and killed a number of sheep, carrying off two, one of which we found buried in the hill-side. In shooting in hilly country it is best to try and keep above a bear, for it is dangerous to shoot at one uphill ; it will come rolling down at great speed and many sportsmen have come to grief in this manner.

But a more dangerous animal is the Himalayan black bear (*Ursus torquatus*). It is often savage, and is prone to attack those who come suddenly on it at close quarters, a common occurrence, as it keeps mainly to bush cover, whereas the brown bear is to be found digging up roots or on the open hill-side turning over stones in search of insects. A brown bear fired at from the crest of a hill charged straight up towards me, but I think it was only a blind rush to escape ;

these animals have poor sight and hearing, and probably no sense of the direction of a sound such as the report of a rifle. A black bear shot in a mulberry tree came down with a bump among bushes, and ran about growling, as though in search of its enemy, until killed by another shot.

The Himalayan black bear is a savage animal, sometimes attacking without provocation, and inflicting horrible wounds, attacking generally the head and face with their claws, while using their teeth also on a prostrate victim. It is not uncommon to see men who have been terribly mutilated, some having the scalp torn from the head, and many sportsmen have been killed by these bears. In one case a man was killed by being first felled by a paw and then having the back of his head nearly bitten off. In 1883 near Dharmsala, a Mr. Knowles was watching a hill-side when a bear came upon him from behind, and, before he could turn, seized him and threw him and itself down a hill 40 feet to the ground; he was picked up dead with a broken skull and the bear disappeared in the bushes. Meanwhile a second bear attacked another of the party, and after receiving two bullets and a gash with a knife, it knocked him down, but he escaped with some bruises. The same animal then attacked a Gurkha officer, bit his thigh, and threw him over a hill into a mountain stream. These bears are generally met with in bush cover, and therefore often at very close quarters, when an animal is more likely to attack in a panic or in an attempt to escape; a brown bear, being met on the open ground in most cases, is less likely to be aggressive, even apart from its probably milder character.

It is curious that bears, furnished with such killing

and flesh-eating armature, should resort so little to a carnivorous diet, while man, equipped rather as a vegetarian animal, should be so greatly addicted to flesh-eating. Some species of bears and some individuals of other species are given to killing and eating animals; the grizzly feeds largely on fish and will eat dead deer and buffalo. The Himalayan black bear has been known to tear a bullock to pieces, or to eat great bits of flesh off the living creature. But generally bears prefer roots, fruit, honey, and insects. Even the polar bear, which feeds largely on seals and other marine animals, is partial to a vegetable diet.

The early explorers, led on by a spirit of adventure and attracted by the glamour of an unknown and mysterious land, braved the icy terrors of the Arctic regions under conditions far more rigorous than those of our time; and some of them added to their account of those terrors apocryphal stories of the ferocity and man-eating propensities of Polar bears. But the bears which pursued the sailors of Barentz probably had no hostile intention. There is no record of the unwounded animals attacking men; bears are generally defensive, not offensive creatures.

The sloth bear, perhaps misnamed for it is by no means slothful either in attack or retreat, is in general a harmless beast, sleeping during the day in caves or under shady trees and bushes, and wandering by night in search of fruit, ants' nests, and honey. But when met with at close quarters, as by natives gathering jungle produce, it often attacks and inflicts severe injuries, while sportsmen have not infrequently suffered from its claws and teeth. I have shot many of these bears, generally in the early morning, for they retire soon after sunrise, and have been charged from a distance of a few yards by a family of three, but when two were shot the third turned and bolted. Another, driven out of bush cover to the crest of a hill, rushed at me with a gruff roar and was killed when 6 feet off with a shot in the head; one with a cub ran past so close that it received a passing kick, while the cub galloped after and scratched the shins of a man who was trying to escape up a tree. These bears can climb trees, which may be seen scored by their claws when there is fruit or honey to be had, and one went up a tree after Inverarity had shot at and wounded it, and was killed 11½ feet from the ground. One charged out of the bushes beside a jungle path before dawn, and came close up to a pony I was riding, but turned and fled after delivering a roar of disapproval. Another visited my camp in the middle of the night, and left within a short distance of my bed, which was in the open, unsavoury but unmistakable evidence of his presence.

People who live in the jungle may be seen with their heads scored by claws, and, immediately after being attacked, with the scalp hanging like a veil over the face. In 1890 some villagers brought to my camp the skin of a bear which had been so badly mauled by a tiger that they were able to finish it off with clubs and stones. The skin showed marks of the tiger's teeth and claws. The bear had a bad reputation, having mauled many people when they were collecting wood in the forest or cutting grass for their cattle. The tables were turned by an old woman in the same neighbourhood who brought Bruin to an ignominious end. Seeing a bear asleep at the bottom of a cliff, she rolled a great rock on to the top of it and killed it.

In attacking a man standing upright, the bear rushes up and rises on its hind-legs with open jaws, and strikes at the head with its paws, which are well armed with long, sharp claws. Colonel R. W. Burton was mauled by one of these animals when he sat down to lunch rather too close to the spot where he had fired at this or another bear. His thigh was bitten and his head got into the animal's mouth, and was scored and bitten by the teeth, one eye being nearly gouged out and the jaw broken. Being a hundred miles from the railway, he had to be carried for two or three days, fed with milk administered through a rolled leaf, for the whole face was temporarily disabled. Surgical operation entailed the removal of a cheek-bone, afterwards carried about as a memento of the occasion.

A well-known Bombay sportsman, Mr. R. Gilbert, was out with a friend in camp in Dharampur State when a man brought news that a villager had been mauled by a sloth bear. They rode to the place, and found the man sitting in a hut, his face torn and hanging in shreds, his head deeply cut with claw-wounds, and his back badly clawed. The man with a little boy was sitting near the path 250 yards from the village when, without provocation, the bear came up behind and attacked him. The boy went for assistance and several men marked the bear and three cubs down in an adjacent jungle, out of which Gilbert beat and shot them. The man died on the second day. This bear had attacked and mauled several other people in the neighbourhood. An old bullet was found encysted in the fore-arm, as well as a large splinter of bone, which had evidently given great pain, for the wound had healed but was full of pus. No wonder the poor beast was fierce in the recollection of injury by man!

Many years ago a young officer was brought into Chicacole, in South India, in a blanket tied to a bamboo. He was grievously wounded when after bears on a hill 20 miles off. While he was poking about among the rocks, a bear slipped out of a cave behind him, upset him in a trice, and chawed up his hands in a frightful manner; two fingers of his left hand had to be amputated, and some bones excised from his wrist; he had protected his face with his hands. The bears in the Canara District of Southern India had a very bad reputation; the natives feared them more than tigers, and indeed when come upon at close quarters a bear is more ready to charge than a tiger. In Canara there were numerous instances of men attacked without provocation, and people carried for their protection bludgeons made of hard and heavy wood from a particular tree; these had to be cut by moonlight in such a manner that the shadow of the axe did not fall on the tree, which was supposed to have occult properties.

In 1915 a native was attacked and scalped at Mount Abu in Rajputana by a she-bear who had with her two half-grown cubs. They left him face down and insensible. He was later found and taken to hospital; the whole of his scalp-cap had gone, shreds hanging over the face and neck. In none of these cases was there any attempt at eating, and in the last instance the bear did not even eat the scalp, which was afterwards picked up on the spot.

Comparatively few of those cases come to public notice, but the loss of life from attacks by bears is considerable. In one year 94 people were killed in

India by these animals; of these 52 were in Bengal and Assam, and 16 in the North-West Provinces and Oudh, where both the Himalayan black bear and the sloth bear are found, so it is not possible to apportion the blame; 22 deaths in the Central Provinces and Madras must have been due to sloth bears. In the Punjab only three people were killed, evidently by the Himalayan species. There were 590 cattle killed by bears in the same year. It is significant that 241 of these were in the Punjab and 214 in Oudh, pointing to the special destructiveness of the Himalayan species, for only 24 were killed in Bengal, and 45 in Madras. It may be concluded that while sloth bears kill more people than Himalayan black bears, the latter are more destructive to cattle.

CHAPTER XVIII

CROCODILES, ALLIGATORS, AND SERPENTS

CROCODILES are among the most horrible and destructive of all man-eaters; Mr. Theodore Roosevelt says in his *African Game Trails*, that they claim more human victims than lions and leopards in Africa, where they appear to be more destructive than in India. Their very method of approach to their prey is repulsive to a degree. They are silent, relentless, horrifying. A man or a woman may be engaged in washing themselves or their clothes in the shallows of a river. Engrossed in this occupation they are unlikely to observe the crown of the monster's head which, perhaps some fifty yards off, rises for a moment to the surface without a ripple, and then sinks as silently back into the depths. Silent and invisible, the monster which has thus marked down its prey approaches under the water; there is splashing as it rushes through the shallows, a scream as the victim is gripped in the iron jaws; the crocodile rushes back sending up spray, cleaves the water and plunges into the depths with its hapless prey. Perhaps a hand and arm may appear for a moment above the surface, and then is gone; the calm wave ripples to the bank, and all is still.

A recent *Gazette* records the award of the Albert Medal to Mr. Leonard Pemberton, who made a gallant attempt to save a boy who was seized by a crocodile on November 14th, 1930. A number of children were bathing in the Zambesi river at Livingstone, a few miles above the Victoria Falls, where a space enclosed for bathing is used by hundreds of people daily in summer. A youth named Van Standen was seen hanging on to the wire of the enclosure, seized by a crocodile, and Mr. Pemberton, fully clothed, dived in, despite the fact that he was convalescing from a recent illness, and made repeated attempts to get the boy from the crocodile, which was holding him under water, but all his efforts failed.

The popular idea that the great carnivorous mammals are all man-eaters applies also to the great reptiles, to sharks, and some other sea monsters. Every individual is supposed to be an actual or at least a potential man-eater. Crocodiles are scavengers; they feed mainly on fish and small mammals, but are ready at all times to eat putrescent animal matter that may find its way into their waters, and animals they kill are left to rot before being devoured; the larder is generally under the bank of rivers or lakes. Crocodiles abound in the waters of India, in other parts of Asia, Africa, and the north coast of Australia, where they sometimes enter the sea. In the New World they are represented by alligators, a genus differing from the crocodile in some structural details.

Crocodiles are of several species, the chief being the gavials, which have long narrow jaws like the elongated beak of a pterodactyl, and inhabit the rivers of Northern India, subsisting chiefly on fish; and the common snub-nosed reptile, addicted sometimes to man-eating, and found throughout India and Ceylon, in other parts of Asia, and in Africa. The gavial attains a length of over 20 feet; the snub-nosed crocodile is seldom more than 15 feet in length. Both are well furnished with formidable teeth. These reptiles may be seen floating like logs in the water, only the eyes and top of the head usually visible, or basking on a sand-spit or on the river bank, when it is sometimes possible to approach within a few yards. Often when basking the jaws are wide open, and the small birds which tend them can be seen hopping in and out, picking up insects as described by Herodotus, who also said that their cry warns the crocodile of danger; but though these birds fly away on approach, they seem to be silent. We used to shoot gavials on the Kabul and Sutlej rivers when out after wild geese and duck; and snub-nosed crocodiles are plentiful in the Mahi river in Baroda territory.

The Mahi river has a sluggish current; we used to embark on a large boat and float down with the stream, aided by the outgoing tide, which came up from the Gulf of Cambay as far as our point of embarkation. One side of the river was overgrown with dense bush down to the water's edge; the other generally bare. On the banks groups of red-headed Sarus cranes uttered their mournful cries; sheldrakes flew overhead, croaking loudly and offering easy shots, but they were not molested, for they are fishy and uneatable, and shots would disturb crocodiles which are very susceptible to the report of a gun. Now and then rough backs and snouts would appear above the surface, where fish often rose to escape their pursuers. Kingfishers blue and pied darted across the stream, at intervals hovering for a moment and dropping plumb to the water to seize a small fish. Crowns and wicked eyes of crocodiles offered tempting shots, but were not taken as, if killed, they would sink to the bottom. The only sure way is to shoot them on dry land, and even then they will escape unless disabled by the first shot. A crocodile rushes into the water at great speed.

On one occasion a large crocodile was hard hit and made a desperate effort to struggle into the water until another shot laid him out. With ropes fore and aft we dragged him in and deposited him at the bottom of the boat, to all appearance dead. We had not gone far when I saw his little eyes shining, and suddenly he became active. Snapping fiercely, he took possession of the boat, the human occupants clambering to comparative safety up the high gunwale. We could not fire again, for a bullet might sink the boat, and snouts appearing above the surface did not invite us to take to the water. We were between the devil in the boat and those in the deep river. At length we managed to run the boat ashore, when a shot in the monster's eye ended his struggles.

Lower down we passed close under the walls of an old fort, fast crumbling into dust, whose turreted battlements rose high above the bed of the stream. Below this more crocodiles were seen and one shot at 80 yards distance; it rolled down a steep bank and, with a splash and a mighty swirl, disappeared under water. We soon found that the carcass lay in a depth of 6 feet; we naturally were not eager to dive in, and it was well that we did not attempt this; we at length managed to lever the crocodile up with a pole, I seized the tail, and hung on to it over the side of the boat, the reptile very much alive and struggling.

However, we got a rope round him behind his hind-legs and hauled him ashore, where he lay with open jaws, apparently *in extremis*, but when a stout bamboo was placed between his teeth his jaws closed on it with enough force to crush it to pieces and to have taken off a man's leg. A bullet in the head settled him. He was 13 feet long.

In the crocodiles' stomachs we found a cat, a duck, the remains of dogs and goats, a bushel of pebbles, swallowed to aid digestion, a small silver coin, and a child's silver bracelet, which pointed to one of them, a 6-footer only, being a man-eater, although none was reported in the neighbourhood. The men who stripped off the hides for tanning at Cawnpore carried away the flesh to eat; it had a horrible gelatinous appearance and a fishy and musky odour. A few dozen eggs, the size of a duck's but with soft leathery, opaque skins, were esteemed a great delicacy.

One would not expect to find crocodiles at Oxford, but Frank Buckland relates that his father, then Canon of Christ Church, in 1829, met in the High Street Black Will, a celebrated coachman who drove the "Defiance"; he was tugging along in each hand a crocodile about four feet in length. The Canon purchased them from Will, who had bought them on speculation in London. The first thing he did was to prove the possibility of turning the crocodile's forelegs backwards, so as to make a sort of bridle, thus confirming that the reptile could be so treated. Put into hot water, one crocodile died and the other lived a few hours. They were dissected at the anatomy school by the late Dr. Kidd, and it was agreed to taste the flesh; many participated, and it was pronounced to be excellent, resembling sturgeon or tunny. But old William, who lived with the specimens in the anatomy school and seems to have resembled some of them in appearance, was made so ill through eating crocodile steak that a doctor had to be called in; he was found clasping his stomach and could only say: "Oh that crocodile! Oh that crocodile!" It turned out that while his masters had only tasted the flesh, he had found it so good that he had made a meal of it. Many a man has died from being eaten by crocodiles, but surely no man has been brought so near death by eating one!

Crocodiles may be shot from an ambush, a dog or goat being tethered near the water as bait; or they may be caught with hook and rope, or harpooned in shallow lakes or tanks. It is related that the moat round the fort at Vellore in the Madras Presidency was full of crocodiles which had been introduced to deter soldiers from breaking out of barracks. Vellore was at one time an important fortress with a garrison of English and native troops. Here a native regiment mutinied in 1806 and killed most of the white garrison, when Colonel Gillespie at the head of the 19th Light Dragoons galloped from Arcot, the scene of Clive's famous defence, blew in the gates with his galloper guns, and suppressed the revolt by the most drastic measures. Had similar resolute action been taken at Meerut on the outbreak in 1857, the Indian Mutiny would not have spread so far, or have had such disastrous results.

However, the soldiers soon learnt that when the morning and evening guns were fired every crocodile sank to the bottom of the ditch, and remained there for some moments until the reverberations of the report died away. So they swam over in safety at night, and returned under cover of the friendly gun in the morning. The crocodiles were protected by a garrison order prohibiting fishing for them, which was done with an arrangement of ropes and hooks harnessed to a goose, while a pariah dog was soundly beaten on the bank to serve as a dinner-bell for the hungry monsters. The subalterns were sometimes allowed to "fish," and the Brigadier had been observed to ensconce himself in an embrasure and so enjoy the sport without forfeiting any of his dignity. The goose was taken by the crocodile in a mighty swirl of water. Twenty minutes were allowed for pouching, and then several men hauled on the ropes and pulled the reptile out of the ditch. Sir Emerson Tennant related that in Ceylon crocodiles were caught on a baited hook attached to a log for a float, just as pike are caught with trimmers in England.

The statistics of people destroyed by wild beasts in India do not show separately the numbers killed by crocodiles; these do not appear to be numerous. In Ceylon an officer of the Survey Department pitched his tent one evening on the dry bed of a tank. He was disturbed at night by a movement beneath his bed, and next day a crocodile came up under the matting on the floor. He might have had a worse experience. In 1861 a young man was washing his face by the waterside when a crocodile emerged from some bushes growing in the water and seized him by the calf of his leg. He caught hold of an overhanging branch, calling for help, and a desperate struggle ensued. At length his uncle, who was in the jungle close by, ran up and belaboured the crocodile with a stick; but it held on grunting at each blow. The uncle drew a knife and stabbed it in the eye and it relinquished hold, but only to seize the victim by the thigh. He then inserted the knife in its jaws and tried to rip it open, and the crocodile let go and slid into the water. The youth was taken to Kaitura, and medical aid was given, but he died from loss of blood.

Crocodiles on the Zambesi are peculiarly destructive, but probably casualties in Africa are largely due to carelessness and the trust put by the natives in charms supposed to render them immune from attack. Mr. Maugham saw two people taken. One was a native in the act of washing in the shallows, and Maugham had turned to make a remark to a friend in whose verandah he was sitting regarding the foolishness of the bather. He wrote, in his *Wild Life in Zambesia*, "as I did so, he uttered an exclamation and leaped to his feet, and I looked back to the river just in time to hear a piteous scream and see a commotion in deep water a few yards out from the river bank—just such an agitation as would be made by some huge fish swimming rapidly towards the centre. This died gradually away, and we realized that the poor fellow had indeed gone for ever. We rushed to the water's edge. There lay a red fez and a small pile of clothing. The wide Zambesi flowed placidly at our feet—and that was all." Another native was swept from the stern of his canoe by a crocodile's tail. A mission boy at Blantyre, seized in the Shiré river, hung on to the branch of a tree and yelled; help came in time. Another taken in the same way was rescued, but died. Escape is rare.

During the Jubaland Expedition in 1898 a crocodile seized Captain Tanner when he was filling his water-bottle at the river. He was dragged in, but succeeded in freeing himself, and regained the shore with the help of some of his men. A sepoy was seized when washing, and a crocodile entered a stockade and took a native soldier. On the Juba river a ferry-boat worked between Gobwein and Giumbo, where the crocodiles were very aggressive, attacking and upsetting the ferry; so the plan was adopted of firing a few shots into the water before starting, on the same principle as the gunfire at Vellore.

The alligators or caymans of the New World resemble the crocodiles in general appearance and habits, the chief differences being in the set of the jaws, the teeth, and the separation of the scales of the neck from those of the back. It is perhaps more timid and less aggressive than the crocodile, but many instances are recorded of its attacking and devouring human beings. It attains much the same size as the crocodile, a maximum of about twenty feet, but Waterton describes an immense one not less than thirty feet long, as estimated by those on board a vessel which it passed slowly on the Orinoco. He describes the noise made by the cayman as "a suppressed sigh, bursting forth all of a sudden and so loud that you might have heard it a mile off." Thomas Belt saw an alligator floating in the San Juan river in Nicaragua that "stretched up its head and gave a bellow like a bull." C. R. Brown refers to their abominable musky smell, "like a deadly miasma round our camp, and finding its way even to our palates."

I observed no smell or bellowing in the marshes of Spanish Town in Jamaica, where alligators were numerous fifty years ago, nor in the crocodile-infested rivers of India. It is a curious reflection that mosquitoes, the propagators of malaria and yellow fever, are more destructive of human life, not only than crocodiles and alligators, but than all the wild beasts in the world. There was in the Spanish Town marshes a miasma more deadly than the reptiles that wallowed in the mud. Those who went snipe-shooting ran more risk from yellow fever, from which Lieutenant Phelips, of H.M. guard-ship *Urgent*, died the day after a visit to the swamp in 1885. Another naval officer, a son of Captain Jellicoe of the Royal Mail, perished from the same disease which had claimed so many victims among the troops that the island was indeed a White Man's Grave.

In November of the same year Lieut. F. M. Gray, an officer of the regiment to which I belonged, the 1st West India Regiment, was stricken one morning with the fatal scourge. A day of tossing with high fever, a night of delirium, broken lips and yellow parchment skin, and then the paroxysm of black vomit heralded the last phase. He was only twenty-five when the sad procession, the firing-party with reversed arms, the coffin covered with the Union Jack, bearing sword and helmet, borne on a gun-carriage, the officers of the garrison, for nearly all of whom the Last Post has since sounded, passed through Up Park Camp, much of which was destroyed by an earthquake not long afterwards. The regiment marched away a month later to embark on the troopship *Tyne* for the even more deadly climate of West Africa, where mosquitoes, worse than man-eaters, took their yearly toll. The march played by the band was " Far Away," and even now that plaintive and well-remembered air comes echoing from the past. How Far Away that day seems now, seen through the vista of more than forty-five long years! And most of those who wound in column through the Camp and along the dusty road to the wharf at Kingston are Far Away indeed, and have marched to that land from which they will never more return.

Alligators, like crocodiles, lie quite still and catch animals that come near them. According to Waterton, they attack an animal on land by knocking it into the water by a blow of the tail, and carry it off before it can recover from the effects; they have been known to attack canoes in the same manner. In olden days alligators and crocodiles were regarded as armour-plated, their skins impenetrable, and vulnerable only through the eye. No doubt it was difficult to kill them with inferior weapons, and it is not surprising to read of bullets glancing off their thick hides. Waterton mentions that he saw an Indian kill one with a bow and arrow, the missile entering the cayman's eye. With a modern rifle they are easily killed, a shot in the neck being especially fatal. The naturalist shot two young ones, 2 feet long, with arrows, and says it was astonishing to see what spite and rage they showed, turning round and biting the arrow when struck, and snapping at those who pulled them out of the water. They were like veal to eat.

Waterton had an arrangement of pieces of barbed wood, made by an Indian, baited, suspended a foot above the water, and fastened by a rope to a stake driven into the sand. It is figured in his book, *Wanderings of a Naturalist*. The dinner-bell was furnished, not by a dog as at Vellore, but by the empty shell of a tortoise beaten with an axe. With this apparatus a cayman 10½ feet long was hooked during the night. The naturalist was determined to have a perfect specimen, so instead of shooting it as the Indians wished, and against their advice, he had the reptile hauled ashore and jumped on its back, turning half round as he vaulted into "the saddle," and so gained his seat with his face in the right direction. He immediately seized its fore-legs, and by main force turned them over its back, so that they served as a bridle. The saurian now began to plunge furiously, lashing the sand with its long and powerful tail. But Waterton sat like Arion on the dolphin, and was out of reach of the tail strokes. The people roared out in triumph, while they dragged the cayman and its rider 40 yards inland. He said that if asked how he kept his seat, his reply was: "I hunted some years with Lord Darlington's fox-hounds." The cayman was now exhausted and quiet, and he tied up its jaws and secured its fore-feet in the position in which he held them. Another struggle was soon overcome, and he then cut its throat. This adventure was ridiculed and disbelieved when Waterton published his book in 1825, much as the stories of the adventures of Louis de Rougement were received seventy years afterwards. It was no doubt for this reason that Canon Buckland tested the legs of the crocodile at Oxford as already related.

There are numerous authentic stories of the man-eating propensities of alligators, and the Indians have many such traditions. Before crossing a creek they take precautions against attack by these reptiles. They cut long sticks, and carefully examine the creek for some distance above and below the point of crossing, and as soon as the boldest has passed over, he examines the other side, and then all follow. Don Felipe de

Yuciarte, Governor of Angostura on the Orinoco, related that one evening the people were sauntering up and down on the Alameda, when a large cayman rushed out of the river, seized a man, and carried him down before anyone could assist him. The screams of the poor fellow were terrible as the cayman was running off with him; but the monster plunged into the river with its prey and they instantly lost sight of him, and never saw or heard him more.

Bates relates that on the Amazon the Indians both fear and despise the great cayman; he joined with a party to enter a shallow lake that swarmed with them, out of which they pulled one 8 feet long, and bound its legs and jaws. Like other man-eaters the cayman does not attack a man when on his guard, but is cunning enough to know when he can be seized with impunity. But a few days afterwards a large cayman appeared in shallow muddy water at Caicara, and they had to be very careful when bathing, as the port and bathing-place lay at the foot of a long sloping bank. A drunken man went down to bathe and stumbled, when "a pair of gaping jaws, appearing suddenly above the surface, seized him round the waist and drew him under the water. A cry of agony 'Ai Jesus!' was the last sign made by the wretched victim. The village was aroused: the young men with praiseworthy readiness seized their harpoons and hurried to the bank; but of course it was too late; a winding track of blood on the surface of the water was all that could be seen. They embarked in boats, determined on vengeance: the monster was traced, and when, after a short lapse of time, he came up to breathe—one leg of the man sticking out from his jaws—was despatched with bitter curses."

In another case a young man was bathing when he was seized by the thigh and carried under water. His father, who was on the bank, rushed after the cayman, which was diving away with its victim. He reached the reptile and forced it to relinquish its booty by thrusting his thumb into its eye. Bates saw the marks of its teeth in the lad's thigh. This method of dealing with an alligator is of special interest, and should be made known to people subject to attack on the Zambesi and elsewhere in places infested by crocodiles. The late Captain Finch-Hatton saved himself, when seized by a crocodile, by thrusting his fingers into its eyes. Belt says that the natives at Juigalpa in Nicaragua told him that alligators were plentiful in the river, but harmless. Everyone bathed without fear, which would not be the case if anyone had been seized in the last fifty years for, as he truly says, " no traditions are more persistent than tales of the attacks of wild beasts." At Greytown he heard several stories of people being killed, but only one was authenticated. The head of the Moravian Mission at Blewfields told him that several youths went to bathe in the river, which was rather muddy at the time. The first to plunge in was a boy of twelve, who was immediately seized by a large alligator and carried along under water. Belt's informant and others followed in a canoe and recovered the body, but life was extinct. The alligator cannot devour its prey beneath the water, but crawls on land with it after he has drowned it.

The naturalist Audubon averred that salt water is poison to alligators, but that they take to the sea at times was proved when one came ashore near the barracks at St. Ann's, Barbados, in 1886. They are not indigenous in that island, and the nearest habitat was believed to be in Trinidad, 200 miles distant.

There are many species of great serpents, the pythons of the Old World, especially plentiful in India and Malaya, the boa-constrictors of America, and the anacondas or gigantic water-snakes of Guiana and Brazil, which abound in the Amazon and its tributaries. In India 20,000 people were killed by poisonous snakes in 1922, but there are few records of human beings destroyed by pythons. These attain to something over 20 feet in length. I saw the track of one across a dusty path in the Nallamallai Hills of Southern India, which was over a foot in width. General E. F. Burton shot one over 17 feet long in the same district, and they are commonly found from 12 to 14 feet long. In 1928 there was a python 25 feet in length in the Zoological Gardens.

These great snakes are not poisonous; they kill their prey by enfolding it with their coils and destroy it by constriction. On the Rampur Ghat in Oudh two boys, roaming in the jungle, suddenly came upon an immense python half hidden in the undergrowth. They did not know what it was, and one of them went to look at it, when the serpent sprang and seized him. The other boy gave the alarm, and the people of a neighbouring village came to the spot. When they first saw the yellow heaving mass among the leaves and grass, they thought it was a leopard, but on going closer they found that the boy was lying in the folds of an enormous snake. On receiving several blows from bill-hooks, the snake began to uncoil, and the villagers dragged the boy away and killed the python, which was over 16 feet long. The boy was quite dead. All his ribs and other bones were more or less broken, and his stomach was burst open by the violence of the embrace.

William Daniell, R.A., an artist who resided ten years in India early in the last century, painted among many other pictures of Indian scenery one illustrating the seizure of a man in a boat by an immense python. The boat, sent into one of the creeks of the Hughli to obtain fruit, was moored under the bank in charge of one of the men. While he was asleep the python coiled itself round him, and would have crushed him to death had not his companions fortunately returned and, attacking the serpent with axes, severed the tail end and released him. They then killed the python, which was said to measure over 62 feet in length. No doubt the imagination was stretched as well as the serpent.

A few instances of human beings killed by the great serpents are recorded from South America, but snakes, like other wild animals, are not generally aggressive towards man. The hamadryad, or king cobra, attaining a length of 14 feet, has been known to attack man, but snakes, poisonous or not, will usually attempt to escape. Waterton truly writes that " it comes to nearly the same thing in the end whether the victim dies by poison from the fangs, which corrupts the blood, or whether his body be crushed to a mummy and swallowed by a python." Even the largest snakes are not difficult to disable with the blow of a cudgel which breaks the back, although one would imagine that a large anaconda would take some killing. Hartwig says that a boa will " engulf a horse and its rider."

The enterprising traveller and naturalist, Charles Waterton, gives an account of his capture of a boa almost as exciting as his encounter with the cayman. This snake was 14 feet long, of a rare species, as thick as a common 24-foot boa. After skinning it he could get his head into its mouth, such was the expansion of its distended jaws. He found the snake near a fallen tree, and after having carefully cut away the twigs and leaves that almost covered it, he exposed its head and pinned it to the ground with a spear-thrust just behind the neck. One of his attendant negroes then held the spear while he grappled with the serpent, getting hold of its tail, and at length overpowered it with the aid of other negroes. It was eventually got into a bag, and, like the cayman, was despatched by having its throat cut. He afterwards captured another 10 feet long, which he knocked out with a blow, and then holding it by the throat with both hands, while it coiled itself round his body, he marched it off to his camp for disposal.

These were small specimens. The anaconda is said to attain a length of 60 feet. Bates says that it grows to enormous bulk and lives to a great age; he heard of specimens 42 feet long being killed. During his voyage up the Tapajos he was awakened in the night by a heavy blow on the side of the boat, and in the morning found the bottom of a hen-coop broken and two fowls taken. The neighbourhood was searched next day and the culprit found sunning itself on a log at the mouth of a rivulet. It was despatched with harpoons, and proved to be an anaconda over 18 feet long and 16 inches in circumference at the widest part. He afterwards measured a skin 21 feet long and 2 feet in girth. The reptile has a hideous appearance, being very broad in the middle and tapering at both ends.

Bates relates that at Ega an anaconda was near making a meal of a ten-year-old boy, who was out with his father gathering fruit. They landed on a sandy shore, and the boy was left with the canoe while his father went into the forest. While the child was playing under the trees a huge anaconda wound its coils round him, unperceived until it was too late to escape. His cries brought his father, who rushed forward, boldly seized the serpent by the head and tore its jaws asunder.

CHAPTER XIX

SHARKS

ON April 2nd, 1885, the Royal Mail steamer *Moselle*, bound for the West Indies and the Spanish Main, left Southampton and steamed down the Channel and out into the Atlantic in fair weather. But before we passed the Azores a heavy sea, clear, green and unbroken, was running high; sails were set to steady the ship or to save steam. Soon the sky darkened and the sea became black as ink; the wind dropped; the clouds were driving in the heavens; there was neither thunder, nor lightning, nor rain. Only the moon appeared at intervals between the torn battalions of the clouds and lit up the now raging sea; for the storm had broken upon us, and the foaming waves with driven mist and spindrift bore down upon the ship. In an instant the sails were rent like muslin and blown away in shreds, leaving their torn fragments flapping forlornly against the masts, while more than one spar snapped and the masts creaked and groaned and seemed about to break. A seaman was blown down the hatchway and killed. But we had a good ship and a good captain; in a few hours the storm abated, we ran out of its orbit, and the vessel floated serene on the great Atlantic swell. We passed a small derelict and dismasted barque, and as I looked over the stern of our ship the ghastly face of a drowned man appeared for a moment in the silver track of the moon and was swiftly borne away on the face of the waters. Next day our dead sailor, sewn up in a hammock with a heavy shot attached, was dropped overboard after a proper funeral—a sad sight to see him go down and down, "still less and less, a speck of white, that gemmed the tide, then mocked the sight."

In due course on the thirteenth day from Southampton, after passing the small island of Sombrero, shaped like a cardinal's hat, we entered the port of St. Thomas, then a Danish island, and lay-to a quarter of a mile from the shore. The harbour is in the shape of a horseshoe, with a narrow entrance, providing a safe anchorage from the stormy seas without. The town, picturesquely built on the slope of a mountain, stretched down to a low, sandy shore; the white houses with their red roofs and green venetian blinds nestled amid the fronds of innumerable palms and bright green banana trees. Round the ship crowded a mass of boatmen contending for hire, and from a dinghy negro diving-boys plunged in to retrieve the small coins thrown into the sea by the passengers.

Being young and unsophisticated I expected to see sharks rise from the depths and come after the boys, for in those days we thought that every shark was a man-eater. But the nigger boys went on merrily in and out of the water, and dived down into the glassy depths as though there were no such thing in the sea as a ravening shark. The boatmen had sharks' jaws for sale, set wide open with several rows of triangular, saw-edged teeth; but that was all we saw of sharks until we were leaving. They were said not to be dangerous in St. Thomas's harbour, perhaps because food from the shipping and the shore was plentiful. But by dragging a dead horse or other animal behind a boat they may be brought up and shot with rifles near the port entrance, as they had been some years before. To make sure, not only was the shark shot as he turned on his back to seize the carcass, but a negro standing ready with a harpoon would drive it home at the same moment, so that the fish could be easily secured and towed off behind the boat. Sharks are very tenacious of life. Audubon records that one caught on board a ship he was on was cut in half, and that the head half swam away out of sight.

I did at last see the back fin of a shark, black and triangular above the surface, as we steamed out of harbour towards a great waterspout that rose in the distance, a tall column like a pillar of dark cloud joining the ocean to the vault of the sky; it collapsed and melted into the sea from which it had risen. But there were plenty of sharks to be seen in the long narrow bay of Port au Prince when, after coasting round the southern shore of Haiti, we entered it on the third day from St. Thomas. They swam round the ship, greedily seizing offal thrown overboard, and it was noticeable that there were here no diving-boys. Perhaps sharks are especially dangerous at Port au Prince. If so, that did not deter the gallant Robert Rollo Gillespie, then a captain in the 20th Light Dragoons, and Captain Rowley, R.N., from swimming ashore under fire with their swords in their mouths and a flag of truce in May 1794, when the place was blockaded by the English fleet. Gillespie escaped the sharks and bore a distinguished part in subsequent operations. But four years later he encountered an even greater danger in

San Domingo, when the place was in English occupation. One night his house was entered by eight desperadoes who murdered his servant. Gillespie, hearing the noise, got up and with his sword attacked the assassins, killed six of them and was dangerously wounded by the other two, who then made their escape. He was a little man, and the fame of his exploit preceded him to England, so that when he was presented at the King's levee, George III said : " What ! is this the little man who killed all the robbers ? " There are many species of shark. Some, such as the Basking Shark found round the English coast, are harmless. The Tiger Shark, attaining a length of 30 feet, is the most dangerous to human beings, but William Beebe, walking in diving-dress on the bottom of Darwin Bay, found that, except for curiosity, they paid no attention to him, although swimming all round and darting at and taking hooked fish. This eminent naturalist of the deep seas " reserves judgment " as to the ferocity of sharks.

It seems probable that sharks will always be ready to attack human beings when driven by extreme hunger, or excited by blood, as of wounded men in battle. But an extraordinary incident took place off Jamaica in 1885. The sharks of Port Royal are perhaps peculiarly savage ; three sailors from the guard-ship *Urgent* went ashore for a spree. They started back after sunset but never reached their ship. Next morning the boat was found floating in the harbour, and in it the mangled corpse of one of the men. His comrades had gone, and it was supposed that the boat had capsized and two of the sailors had been taken by sharks, while the third managed to right the boat and scramble back into it, only to die from his wounds. We used to see plenty of sharks on the way to visit the guard at Fort Augusta at the harbour mouth, where the artillerymen sometimes fished for them. And they were to be seen also near Rock Fort on the shore by the Palisadoes, famous in bygone days as the resort of pirates and buccaneers, who held high revel until their stronghold was destroyed by an earthquake. We saw sharks, too, in Carlisle Bay, Barbados, deep down in the emerald depths, where the branching coral grows, and where we could see porcupine fish, and great skates, and giant crayfish. At times flying fish, chased by bonitos and perhaps by sharks and barracoutas, would rise from the waves and wing their way over the surface, to drop like a silver shower into the sea.

The most vivid account of a shark tragedy is given in Michael Scott's *Tom Cringle's Log*. This took place off Moro Castle in the Bay of Santiago di Cuba. Tom Cringle relates that "a very melancholy accident happened to a poor boy (of the gunboat *Firebrand*) of about fifteen years of age, who had already become a great favourite of mine from his modest quiet deportment, as well as of all the gunroom officers, although he had not been above a fortnight in the ship. He had let himself down over the bows by a cable to bathe. There were several of his comrades standing on the forecastle looking at him, and he asked one of them to get out on the spritsail yard and look round to see if there were any sharks in the neighbourhood; but all around was deep, clear, green water. He kept hold of the cable, however, and seemed determined not to put himself in harm's way, until a wicked little urchin, who used to wait on the warrant-officers' mess—a small meddling snipe of a creature, who got flogged in well-behaved weeks only once—began to torment my mild little favourite.

"'Why, you chicken-heart, I'll wager a thimbleful of grog that such a tailor as you are in the water can't for the life of you swim out to the buoy there.'

"'Never you mind, Pepperbottom,' said the boy, giving the imp the name he had richly earned by repeated flagellations. 'Never you mind—I am not ashamed to show my naked hide, you know. But it is against orders in these seas to go overboard, unless with a sail under foot; so I shan't run the risk of being tattooed by the boatswain's mate like someone I could tell of.'

"'Coward,' muttered the little wasp, 'you are afraid,' and the other boys abetting the mischief-maker the lad was goaded to leave his hold of the cable and strike out for the buoy. He reached it, and then turned and pulled towards the ship again, when he caught my eye.

"'Who is that overboard! How dare you disobey the standing order of the ship? Come in, boy, come in.'

"My hailing the little fellow shoved him off his balance, and he lost his presence of mind for a moment or two, during which he, if anything, widened his distance from the ship. At this instant the lad on the spritsail-yard sang out quick and suddenly, 'A shark, a shark!' And the monster, like a silver pillar, shot up perpendicularly from out the dark green depths of the sleeping pool, with the waters sparkling and hissing around him, as if he had been a sea-demon rushing upon his prey.

"'Pull for the cable, Louis,' shouted fifty voices at once—'pull for the cable.'

"The boy did so—we all ran forward. He reached the cable—grasped it with both hands, and hung on, but before he could swing himself out of the water, the fierce fish had turned. His whitish-green belly glanced in the sun—the poor little fellow gave a heart-splitting yell, which was shattered amongst the impending rocks into piercing echoes, and these again were reverberated from cavern to cavern, until they died away among the hollows in the distance, as if they had been the faint shrieks of the damned—yet he held fast for a second or two—the ravening tyrant of the sea tug, tugging at him till the stiff, taut cable shook again. At length he was torn from his hold, but did not disappear; the animal continuing on the surface crunching his prey with his teeth, and digging at him with his jaws, as if trying to gorge a morsel too large to be swallowed, and making the water flash up in foam over the boats in pursuit by the powerful strokes of his tail, but without ever letting go his hold. The poor lad only cried once more—but such a cry—oh, God, I shall never forget it!—and, could it be possible, in his last shriek, his piercing expiring cry, his young voice seemed to pronounce my name—at least, so I thought at the time, and others thought so too. The next moment he appeared quite dead. No less than three boats had been in the water alongside when the accident happened, and they were all on the spot by this time. And there was the bleeding and mangled boy, torn along the surface of the water by the shark, with the boats in pursuit, leaving a long stream of blood, mottled with white specks of fat and marrow in his wake. At length the man in the bow of the gig laid hold of him by the arm, another sailor caught the other arm, boat-hooks and oars were dug into and launched at the monster, who relinquished his prey at last, stripping off the flesh, however, from the upper part of the right thigh until his teeth reached the knee, where he nipped the shank clean off, and made sail with the leg in his jaws.

"Poor little Louis never moved once after we took him in."

More fortunate in these seas was Sir Brooke Watson, who, when a youth, was swimming near his ship when he saw a shark making for him. He at once shouted for help, and a rope was thrown and he managed to reach it, but while the men were hauling him in the shark tore off his leg. A story is related in Hughe's *Natural History of Barbadoes*, that in the reign of Queen Anne a merchant ship arrived at Barbados from England. Some of the crew were swimming when a large shark swam towards them, but all reached the ship safely except one who was bitten in two. A comrade vowed vengeance, and with a sharp-pointed knife in his hand plunged into the water, and as the fish turned up towards him stabbed it repeatedly in the belly. He then dragged the shark ashore, ripped open the stomach, and afterwards buried the trunk of his friend's body in the same grave as the remaining half.

In the South Seas sharks are regarded as " relations " by the islanders, who have been known to swim about after dynamited fish in company with and unmolested by sharks employed in the same pursuit. And a man has drifted all night unharmed in a shark-infested sea.

Travellers to the East have seen the sharks at Suez and Aden. In the Gulf of Suez they attain a large size, and some fine ones were caught from the P. & O. mail steamer in March 1901, when anchored for a time awaiting the passage through the canal of the *Ophir* with the King (then Duke of York) on board. The teeth, prized by the natives as charms, were much in demand by the ship's passengers. At Aden there were some years ago many diving-boys, one of whom had a leg taken off by a shark; the incident was photographed by a passenger on the mail steamer, and after that the diving was stopped.

Fish form the chief food of sharks. Darwin relates that the balloon-fish, Diodon, has often been found floating alive and distended in the stomach of a shark, and that it will eat its way not only through the stomach coats but through the sides of the monster, which is thus destroyed. Other fish besides sharks have an evil reputation. Of these the barracouta is certainly dangerous, for it is apt to seize the extremities of a man swimming. It was numerous off St. Ann's, Barbados, where we used to discharge a rifle into shoals of mullet from the end of the engineer's pier; but we kept a look-out for sharks and barracoutas before diving in to gather up the stunned fish.

In those seas there is also the giant ray, commonly called the devil-fish, a name sometimes applied to the octopus. But the devil-fish is harmless, and satanic only in appearance. The great octopus also has an unmerited evil reputation, due to the stories of ancient mariners, and perhaps still more to writers of fiction, who have much to answer for in libelling wild creatures. The octopus is a horror with its protruding eyes and its repulsive tentacles flowing like a dark viscid fluid, or like snakes slipping along, but it has not been known to attack man outside the pages of Victor Hugo's *Toilers of the Sea* and tales of less eminent authors. Many were washed ashore on the coast of the Gallipoli Peninsula in 1915, victims of the war at sea.

INDEX